THE CUSTODIAN
CHRONICLES, VOLUME 1

THE CUSTODIAN CHRONICLES, VOLUME 1

an inside look at the american public school
system as seen through the eyes of its most
underrated player: the janitor (and other musings)

Tim Will Hunting

For the rebels, the folk devils, and those who never settle—
be *you*, be *here*, be *now*.

Contents

Acknowledgments

There are a plethora of people without whom this book might never have seen the light of day. Let me begin by thanking anyone and everyone with whom I have ever crossed paths inside the public school system, not only during my times of employment but also as a young child and teenager. While I did not know it at the time, your input, influence, and individual personalities would go on to stoke the fire inside me that has manifested itself in this book and the rest of my creative endeavors. My fifth-grade gym teacher wrote a single word in my yearbook: Perseverance. Thank you, Mrs. Kern, for teaching me the most valuable lesson I could learn, and also for teaching me how to ride a unicycle.

Thanks to all those who spent their hard-earned money on helping me attain this vision. I am eternally grateful and humbled by your generosity. The online community that we share together is something I appreciate and learn from, and for that I am a lucky man.

Thank you to my brother and sister, to whose brains and intellect I could never hold a candle. You two are the smartest goofballs I know. It hasn't always been easy, but we are here, and we are stronger than ever.

Thanks to the children in my life who challenge me, lift me up, drive me crazy, and make me believe in my own sense of self. I am not always easy to figure out, but it's my job to keep you on your toes and guessing. To the one I call "Fish," for your unbelievably compassionate heart, to my "Ewok," for your innate ability to make me smile even on my worst days, and to "Neckbone," who is the perfect mixture of brave and timid, constantly forcing me to set the example that a good man should. I am forever changed by the three of you.

Thank you to my dear friend Melissa Ann Oliverio-Gilbert, the reading teacher who connected it *all*. The one who read through all my crazy ideas as they came to fruition and the one who convinced me that the work I do is relevant, that my mind is strong, and that my job will never truly define me, but it will inspire me to try to create something great. Don't worry! That young boy of yours is going to conquer the world, and eventually Kate will speak to me.

For my parents, who taught me the true meaning of family: unconditional, unwavering loyalty, no matter how much heartache and pain. It took a long time, but it's nice to simply talk and laugh now.

To my musical brothers in arms, who have made my lifelong dream of being in a kick-ass band come true. Words can't express how thankful I am for the times we have shared, the music we have created, and the people we have inspired. We are just getting started! "I couldn't stay at home, I had to break free, my brothers by my side, and so they take me." We are simply Shamans on Saturn.

R. Smalls, for holding me down since day one and for being the definition of what a best friend should be. Ten percent of ten million, homey.

Thank you, Kaa, for taking the time to read, edit, and give me your expert advice, even with a houseful of amazing children who require your utmost motherly attention. Your input got me out of a creative rut and assured me I could see this through. On a side note, your husband is one of the smartest and coolest people I know. To the Nanster, the Tuckster, and the rest of the clan, see ya on the North Fork!

To my other set of parents, my numerous aunts and uncles from the Huether side of the family. You've made my life so worth it! Thank you for the love and support. To my Grandpa, Maximo Maglaya. I hope I represent the Almeida name with dignity.

To the activists I have crossed paths with, walked side by side with, prayed with, and fought with. The truth cannot be denied. Keep up the good fight! To the house dance and hip-hop community worldwide, thank you for harnessing my energy at a young age and molding me into a more connected and cultural individual. To my brothers and sisters in the martial arts scene, the same goes for you. Words can't express how much you have helped me evolve. I love every single one of you. See you on the mats!

To the dreadlocked warrior in Venice Beach, thank you for showing me who I really am all those years ago and teaching me how to let go. And to *la gemela*, my Virgo *hermana* with the revolutionary voice, you speak truth even when no one is listening. Thanks for the guidance over the years. See ya soon.

Last, to my imperfectly perfect better half, the only woman on the planet who gives me a run for my money and keeps me coming back for more. Your support is tried and true, your spirit is pure, and your words stick to my heart and mind. You have always believed in what I am trying to accomplish, no matter how difficult or impossible it may seem. I hope I can provide you the option of early retirement, because you are one teacher I know who surely deserves it. You are certainly a tiny cricket with a loud chirp, and it's the chirp that I adore.

Tin*man: one with no heart

—*Urban Dictionary* definition

My son, James, was three years old when I switched schools for the third time in my teaching career. He was stuck on *The Wizard of Oz* at this time in his little life, obsessed with that scrappy man made out of all types of metal, who clanked around rigid, squeaky, rusted, and full of character. We ate, breathed, and lived daily life revolving around that Tinman for a few years. It was hot, sweaty, and dusty during this particular move. My last school was beginning to close due to declining enrollment, and somehow, fortunately, I was allowed to ride along on my principal's coattails for a different adventure in a new building.

Boxes upon boxes of history were transported from one building to another. Eighteen years of teaching materials had accumulated by 2011. Eighteen years of "stuff." James was helping, sort of, breaking down the cardboard carriers, and as he was busily, happily destroying them, one of the most vital team players found in every school setting dropped in to see how all the chaos was going. I turned to James, who was now ripping and shredding those boxes, and attempted to introduce him to Timmy, our friendly neighborhood cleaner/custodian. In all the mayhem, James, who was actually now making more work for this poor guy to clean up after we did our day's damage, turned and said, "Mom, what's his name? What did you say? Did you say Tinman?"

Giggles galore, along with some snorting, rang through my room, and after a little explaining, all was understood. But the name stuck, and Timmy will forever be Tinman to my very colorful and charismatic son. We call him as such when speaking with or about him. Although the definition defines him as being "one with no heart," when you get to know Timmy, Tim, Tinman, you begin to learn he does not conform to things like rules or definitions. He truly is a thinker and a dreamer, so much more than what a job label defines someone as, and he most certainly is not someone without a heart.

As I have gotten to know Tinman during the years that have followed, I have found, as with most people, their jobs do not ultimately define who they are as a person, nor should they ever.

Merriam-Webster clearly defines the word *custodian* as a caretaker, guardian, and janitor.

But the label of custodian, the definition, is so much more complicated and diversified than we can define by just three simple words. First ideas and preconceived notions produce images where individuals can be quick to judge based on occupation.

Quite frankly, I take issue with stereotyping in general. I do not like it; I feel it is narrow-minded, limited, and arrogant. I take issue with how certain individuals are treated differently based on their employment. People most likely react more favorably to people whose professions are associated with thoughts of being higher-level, skill-based opportunities. I myself have been guilty of it, but shame on me. Shame on all of us. I have seen how people react and relate to the men I have worked with through the years who are custodial workers in school buildings. I do not always like what I see. Mind you, I love people. I listen closely when someone speaks and have genuine thoughts, intentions, concerns, and feelings toward the people I work with every day. All of them, regardless of their titles. Who am I to judge? I am no better or worse than anyone because of my job title, and I like to know who people are underneath the front they present.

As far as custodians go, on one hand, you can find the crotchety man (mostly) who yesses you to death while you plead for help with hammers, ladders, lightbulbs, fadeless backing paper, photocopying paper, toilet paper, paper towels, desks for new students, flooding sinks, flooding toilets, busted pipes, busted burners, vomit, and yes, even poop. A custodian's job is never pretty, cushy, smooth, uninterrupted, or gratifying.

You then have atypical custodians. The diamonds in the rough, the porcupines on the outside who may grumble, grovel, and goad sometimes, and yet on the inside they always do the right thing, and they do it well. They run tight buildings, like ships, cross their t's, dot their i's, make their lists, cross off what's completed, make new lists. They do, do, do, and run smooth, efficient businesses.

Did I say business? Hmmm, yes, I did. I would say the custodians are probably the most important people in the buildings, the schools. They are the ones who open up the business and yes, the ones who close it down. Hmmm, did I say business again? Yes, I did. If you think for a moment that education has not become one of the biggest businesses in this country, maybe you should think again. I am not typically opinionated in nature, but I have been involved with school and education on both sides of the desk my entire life. I have seen education change, the perspective of it change, the students change, and the teachers change. I do not think change is good or bad; it just is.

Tinman happens to be one person who does not fit the standard mold of a custodian in any way. To know him is to know what makes him a person, not just what defines him in a job title. To know him is to know his love for music, people, literature, family, ecofriendliness, and life in general. I happen to love his gift of using words to communicate those thoughts that swirl around in that head of his. It is always a positive thing to walk away from him with a quote from a song or from an article he has read or with a question he may have asked. He is multifaceted, dynamic, talented, and vivid. He most certainly is not a standard school custodian, and as I see it, his current job title is just a rest stop leading to a different road, a better opportunity, and a less restrictive environment meant just for him. I am glad to be his friend.

Jobs, most times, are what we do to make money in order to subsidize a living. I've always found it to be shallow when I'm introduced to someone who responds, "Hi! And what do you do?" As if the job itself tells you about people, who they are, what they are made of. Yes, I understand that it's an icebreaker question, leading into more, possibly deeper conversations. But dear God, there are a million other questions to ask someone you meet for the first time, no? Tell me people do not think differently about someone based on a job label. I just do not like it. Yes, we are all a part of our job, but our job does not define us; it does not rule who we are as individuals. People are people, made up of so many different things, and I would much rather look into someone's eyes and "see" them, find out who they are on the inside, rather than place more weight on what they do for a living. Just saying.

Well now, I have given you a somewhat abridged mouthful of some parts of this story, before it has even begun. I leave the rest of this very debatable conversation up to the Tinman.

Never judge a book or a person by the cover. You may be missing out on something, someone, who is very important, unexpected, and truly extraordinary.

Melissa Ann Oliverio-Gilbert
April 2015

Introduction

A s a writer, I feel it is my job to evoke emotions and create an atmosphere in which readers can ponder questions that they normally wouldn't. I also feel it is the readers' job to decide how they will allow those emotions to affect them and if what I am conveying is something they are willing to consider as possibilities. In our daily lives, all things in this present reality should be open to personal reflection. By practicing nonattachment to beliefs, we can open up doors that we never knew existed. Maybe *The Custodian Chronicles* will help you expose a hidden entrance into the education system, one that you never knew existed, one that only a janitor has the key to. It is my wish that this book will excite and inspire and most important, make you laugh at this peculiar thing we call life. We tend to take ourselves more seriously than we should, and our obsession with making everything a personal matter often gets in our way of some good old-fashioned laughs. I can assure you that nothing is personal until our minds decide to make it so, and the very notion of being offended directly relates to whatever pain we have stored in our minds from our pasts.

This book has been a long time coming, maybe even a few lifetimes. It started out as a simple outlet, a way for me to entertain myself while letting out some steam; an escape. Over the past few years, my rants to my keyboard have slowly morphed into something perhaps a bit more lucid and thought-out, and they have given me the opportunity to be excited about a job that is far from exciting. At the very least, when my shift ends,

I know I will have something to go home and write about. I crafted this book on my dinner breaks and coffee breaks and late at night when I got home from work. I spent the last few years jotting down lines and ideas on Post-it Notes that I would snag from teachers' desks so as not to lose the thoughts that were surfacing. I would grab my phone and e-mail myself ideas as they made their way through my brain like a locomotive on mescaline, and yet, there was also a period of time in which I didn't write anything for months on end, too frustrated to even put my thoughts down clearly. I was terrified at the idea of working the same job for the next twenty-five years, a job that can be disheartening and downright infuriating at times. Still, I've managed to hang in there, forcing myself to see the brighter side of things even when the toilet bowl that I am cleaning does its best to cast a shadow over my optimism.

The Custodian Chronicles has given me the chance to see how far I can push myself as a writer and to see just how many of those whispering voices in my head I can quell in order to manifest their incessant ramblings into something worth reading. This book has allowed me, I hope, to give you, the reader, something to laugh about, get mad about, be disgusted about, be excited about, and be motivated by. Above all else, I hope it will allow you to experience exactly what and how I was feeling when I was transcribing it and perhaps see the education system and life from an angle that you have never been offered.

Some of this was bred from the sheer angst of working an utterly mundane job, which I know is something many people can identify with, feeling trapped in something I never signed up for but have been forced to play. Other parts of this were written strictly from the heart and soul of someone who was raised in the suburban outskirts located only twenty-something miles from one of the greatest cities on the planet, a big reason it conveys that amazingly condescending and raunchy attitude that only we "New Yawkers" know so well. And yet other parts were written from the mind and the spirit of a father and artist, activist and fighter, lover and friend. My goal was simply to pour all my emotion into this at any given time, maybe even recklessly, just to see what would happen when I came out on the other side.

I truly believe in our individual paths. The journey is yours and yours alone. Self-love and positive, healthy emotion are the key to living a fulfilled and balanced life, and my intention was to scatter those themes throughout this book so that you don't lose sight of what really matters in this short and fragile existence. It has been an incredible learning experience. I have come to see that I am, in some aspects, subconsciously hypocritical and flawed and have a lifetime's worth of work to complete for my own personal development. Deep down inside, I truly care about humanity, about our future, about creating peace; and although I sometimes have my very human moments of negativity and hurt, at the end of the day, I want nothing more than for all of us to be *one* family, united.

I believe that we can change anything we want through communication, patience, and a mutual respect for our human identities, and I believe that we need to teach our children about these tenets first and foremost, because as we all know, you can be the smartest person on the planet, but if you're an asshole, nobody worth your time is going to give a shit about how many problems you've solved or how much money you've made.

Thanks so much for taking the time to check out my work. I appreciate *you* with all of my conscious self. With that said, I'd like to welcome you to the life of a janitor via *The Custodian Chronicles*. Enjoy the ride and do your best not to take it too seriously *or* too personally. Love you!

Timothy Almeida Jr.

1

Pissy Walls and Dirty Halls

Most people look at cleaning shit-filled toilets as if it were on par with contracting the bubonic plague or being diagnosed with stage 3 colon cancer. For the most part, when I tell someone that I am a custodian, his or her response usually goes something like this:

> **Person:** So, what do you do for a living?
> **Me:** I'm a custodian.
> **Person:** Oh, cool. Is that a union job?
> **Me:** Yeah. Civil service at its finest.
> **Person:** That's a great job. But you have to clean toilets and shit, right?
> **Me:** Yep. And piss too.
> **Person:** Oh, that kinda sucks.
> **Me:** It's not that bad.

To be honest, once you get past the clogged toilets, the feces stains spread all over the walls by a fifth grader (yes, this happens often, and yes, there is a chance it was your kid) the piss on the floor, the piss in the radiator, the turd in the urinal, the shit-stained toilet paper piled up two feet high *next* to the toilet and not in it, the soap thrown and smeared on every wall and stall partition, the paper towels deliberately thrown on the floor next to the empty garbage can, the pencils and juice boxes and sandwiches and bloody tampons that clog the toilet so bad that even the

USS *Intrepid* couldn't navigate through the flood it causes, cleaning it up becomes second nature. It's like riding a bike or brushing your teeth. Or going to the bathroom, for that matter!

It is inside this second nature, that space where thinking shuts off and the subconscious takes over, that you can find plenty of time to ponder why these institutional bathroom facilities, better known as "gang" bathrooms to us custodians, are in such dire straits. With each splash of brown water that jumps out to attack the flesh of your arms—and sometimes, if you're really lucky, even finding its way to your face—the questions arise...

1. What on God's green earth would drive a child to squat down and take a shit in the middle of the floor?
2. Does anyone even notice how many times the same kid goes to the bathroom in a single day, and isn't it most likely that it is the same select group of children displaying such unconscious and irrational behavior on a daily basis? I would like to believe it is a small percentage of kids, but it seems to get worse and worse with each passing day, which leads me to believe that more and more children are fed up and, sadly, not interested in what the public school classroom has to offer. They'd much rather go hang out in the bathroom and hurl wet paper towels at one another's faces, or better yet, lock each bathroom stall door from the inside and then crawl under the door through a puddle of piss to get out, only so the next kid can't get in. Yes, it's possibly your kid who does this also. I know, I know. Your child would never do that, right? Yeah, mine neither.
3. Are students really so bored and frustrated that they have to take out their frustrations by demonstrating the same behaviors that a three-month-old puppy or a mental patient would?
4. Does anybody even care that kids are spreading shit art like Picasso all over the walls, or is it easier to take the "not my job, not my problem" approach? How can we be teaching our children

the value of compassion and empathy if we as educators, administrators, aides, social workers, and *yes*, even custodians, don't demonstrate it ourselves?

It often seems the general attitude is that most teachers are so overwhelmed with things inside the classroom, having to worry about whatever goes on outside of the classroom is a near-impossible task. With each passing year, the bureaucracy of federal, state, and local education departments grows more and more absurd, and students, teachers, and taxpayers are left to scramble with an education model that, quite honestly, makes no goddamn sense at all.

We need to have a serious look in the mirror and ask ourselves whose fault it is that children are acting this way. Often enough, if you ask parents why their child is doing poorly, they will say, "It's the goddamn teacher." Ask teachers, and they'll say, "It's the goddamn parents." Ask students, and they will blame other students, or the teachers, or their parents! It's the human blame game. *It's not my fault; it's yours! My kid got a failing test score? Well, the teacher must suck! That kid never finishes his homework, his parents must suck even more!* Everyone just blames, blames, blames, year after year after year. It never changes. And why should it? It seems apathy is humanity's best friend when accountability is required. Let me just pass the buck until I kick the bucket, and I'll teach my kid to do the same. It's a cyclical disease that needs to be cured. Luckily for us, the greatest medicine of all is love, and it is absolutely *free*! Except at Walmart, where it's probably on sale.

The idea of healthy self-love, in which individual human beings learn to value their own lives and establish a sense of common decency and self-worth, is one that is severely lacking within the school system as a whole. Surely there are some teachers who understand the value of helping students create their own philosophical foundation based on kindness for others and mutual respect, but too often the public-education model keeps children outwardly focused—or disoriented, depending on how you look at it—and it does not allow them to devise the proper game plan to approach their understanding of self. If we can figure out a way to insert this notion into our curriculum, then surely future generations can and will benefit from it greatly. Preach on, Mr. Preacher Man.

I am the David Copperfield of the custodial
world. I make shit disappear.

From: Almeida, Timothy
Sent: Thursday, October 09, 2014, 9:02 p.m.
To: Teachers
Subject: Bathrooms

Good day, beautiful earthlings. I know that many of you are overwhelmed and busy, so I will make this as quick as I can. If possible, can you please have a talk with your students about proper bathroom etiquette? To say that they are deplorable is an understatement. The second-floor boys' room is being flooded every week. The boys stuff paper towels in the urinal drains and then proceed to jam the handle down so the water flows and flows until a river runs through it, only Brad Pitt does not make an appearance to go fly-fishing in this film. On most days, there are also puddles of urine next to the toilets, as well as underneath the radiator, which means they are either going to the bathroom in it or on it. You say tomato, I say tomahto! The girls' rooms and boys' rooms throughout the building consistently have paper towels and toilet paper strewn about the floors like Mardi Gras, only there are no beads or fun masquerade masks to be found. And to be blunt, many times kids wipe after doing their business, but opt to drop the toilet paper on the floor *next* to the toilet and not inside it. They also enjoy taking the soap from the soap dispenser and spreading it on the walls and floors like finger paint. The second-floor boys are keen for taking the orange air refresher that sticks to the wall and throwing it *in* the toilet, and wet paper towels are on the ceilings on a regular basis. But hey, at least there is no one throwing apples at the walls like they did last year. And apparently, flushing the toilets after use is *soooo* last year that no one even bothers. Who remembers when their parents would say, "If it's yellow, let it mellow, if it's brown…" Ha-ha-ha, I mean LOL…my bad. Anyway, I think proper bathroom use is a key ingredient to leading a fulfilling and thoughtful life, so let's make leaders out of these kids! All right, happy Friday, ya'll. Keep it in the *now*.
Timothy Almeida Jr.
Master of the Custodial Arts
Est. 1978

PS—During extra help at lunch, please ask the kids to take whatever left-over liquid they have in whatever it is they are drinking, and pour it down the sink before putting it in the garbage. Those garbage bags are not meant to retain liquid. Plus, it will teach them another valuable life skill: don't make your school custodian's life more depressing than it already is. I joke, I joke, I kid, I kid! Thanksssss.

People say, "I want peace."

Remove the "I" (ego)

And the "want" (desire)

And find...*peace*...Ahh. Ain't life grand?

Dear Teacher,

It is seven degrees out. This building was built in 1950-something. Some rooms are going to be warmer than others. There will be a bit of a draft from time to time. I'm sorry your room is only a measly sixty-eight degrees. I'll do my best to appease you and get your room to a perfect seventy-two, or if you want, we can make it 102 degrees and do some Bikram yoga together. That way I can find my center again and not wig out over the incessant complaints of it being too cold or too hot inside. Also, a long time ago, someone invented this practical thing called a sweatshirt. It's good stuff. You can borrow one from me if you'd like. Don't take offense at this, either. I'm breaking your chops while providing some clarity, but still, consider what I'm saying. Imagine you were homeless and sleeping on top of a subway grate to stay warm tonight. A little perspective goes a long way. Love ya! Gotta go! Someone needs me to knit an afghan to use in the month of February.
Always,
Tim Will Hunting

2

An Extremely Brief History on the History You Were Most Likely Never Given the Option to Explore

In our dream we have limitless resources, and the people yield themselves with perfect docility to our molding hand. The present educational conventions fade from our minds; and, unhampered by tradition, we work our own good will upon a grateful and responsive rural folk. We shall not try to make these people or any of their children into philosophers or men of learning or of science. We are not to raise up among them authors, orators, poets, or men of letters. We shall not search for embryo great artists, painters, or musicians. Nor will we cherish even the humbler ambition to raise up from among them lawyers, doctors, preachers, statesmen, of whom we now have ample supply.

—FREDERICK D. GATES, BUSINESS ADVISER TO JOHN D. ROCKEFELLER SR., 1923

It is not my intention to bore you with facts and statistics and filler bullshit that will make this book any longer than it needs to be. Many times a "fact" is exaggerated one way or another in order to better serve an

9

agenda or to make an argument more or less relevant. It is also often tainted with the sticky residue of one's own opinion and, as that old saying goes, opinions are like assholes—everyone's got one, but not everyone wipes theirs clean every day!

Now, let's say for argument's sake—meaning I want you to argue with someone you love over what I mean by this—that facts can be seen in two ways. The first one is a fact of actuality. For example, a bird flies, and a monkey throws its own doody—both indisputable facts. The second one is a fact of convenience—some dude is trying to pick up a girl in da club, and he tells her he owns his own company, only it's really his dad's company that he will someday inherit, unless of course he screws it all up by pitching facts of convenience to customers as well. It is kinda sorta a fact that he owns his own company, and it is also kinda sorta bullshit, but it is a convenient "fact" for him when he's trying to get a girl to go home with him. Capisce?

The point is this: facts and opinions are intertwined and twisted so often that the actual truth behind a lot of things is completely skewed. How often do we really think about where facts and information come from before regurgitating then to our friends and family? Most of us have been trained to simply accept without question information given to us and then state it as fact. From as far back as we can remember, both consciously and subconsciously, we are inundated with information, images, symbols, sounds, words, events, places, and people. Lions and tigers and bears, oh fucking my! Infinite gigabytes of data downloaded to our cerebral hard drive. In today's world, the Internet has literally taken its position at the top of the factual food chain. We are suddenly left to deal with a population of professional know-it-alls who spew their newly learned knowledge as if they're the next Nobel laureates. Trust me, I know. This book is a testament to that.

Technological advances make it a brilliant and dangerous time to be alive, and we must start to navigate our human circuit board with more than just a smartphone. We must allow natural evolution to coexist with scientific advancement and technology, without paying too much attention to one or the other. Our children must learn the worth behind the greatest treasure ever revealed: self-knowledge and introspective discovery. And that my friends, is a fact of actuality.

Do we (and I say we because as an adult who is also raising kids, I feel that we are all responsible in some way for not only our own children but one another's as well) constantly spit out information as fact and make our children believe it too? Furthermore, once we set this belief into motion, do kids even have a chance to learn the importance of clear, critical thinking? Can they ever unlearn what they have learned? For example, instead of teaching elementary-school students that Christopher Columbus "discovered" America (a fact of convenience that we all know is complete bullshit once we grow up into brilliant adults), what if we did the following?

Say for a moment we presented "facts" to the students like so:

Teacher: Some people would argue that Christopher Columbus did not discover America because upon arriving, he was met by thousands of natives who were already occupying and cultivating this land successfully. What other possibilities do you think might have happened at this time and even more important, why?

Students' Brains: Neurons firing, brain chemistry activated, beautiful young minds opening to receive free thought, flux capacitor fluxing, possibilities endless! Excitement, participation, intellectual revolution!

Versus:

Teacher: Christopher Columbus discovered America!

Students' Brains: Christopher Columbus discovered America. Fact. What's next?

Don't students deserve the chance to evolve into more than one-dimensional thinkers? The quote at the beginning of this chapter serves as a reference point as to why, over the one hundred plus years of public school education, we seem to have made little progress, and by most counts, have devolved rather than evolved. Allow me to briefly, and I mean briefly, delve into history for a moment, or as some may see it, his-story. I promise I'll make this as entertaining as cleaning the same hallway day after day after day after day...

It has been said that sometime around 1903, John D. Rockefeller Sr. founded the General Education Board. Some historians say it cost about $129 million to implement, which is a shit ton of money even now, so imagine the power that it wielded then. The General Election Board was supposedly created to do one thing, and that was to promote the state-controlled public school movement. Its main goal was to create reliable, predictable, and obedient civilians. Take a moment to yourself. Really, really, really ponder this. Think about your public school experience and ask yourself why we are taught from the very beginning that the state and the president and this country and this flag and our government are always to be idolized rather than questioned. Yes, I know what you're thinking, and the answer is no, I'm not a dirty hippie, militant communist, God-hating sinner who despises America! To be quite frank, I find the idea of countries rather silly and outdated but have yet to think up a better option. Claiming that our piece of dirt is greater than someone else's piece of dirt seems to be something deeply rooted in us. Just as animals claim their territory, we do the same, although if we chose to, we could find the mental capacity to see through this inherently dangerous trait in order to find peaceful solutions that lead to balanced cohabitation.

If this system was indeed created by extremely wealthy politicians and bigwigs to create a subservient population, then why would the agenda be any different in the present day? I mean, for Christ's sake, it's not any different, is it? Aren't we all raised to believe in it—the Machine, the System, the Man? We are bombarded with words like patriotism and hero and war and freedom and allegiance and vote and democracy and phrases like "greatest country in the world" and "Army Strong" and "The few, the brave, the proud," and yet, if we attended public school, we never got a chance to decide for ourselves, nor do our kids get a chance to decide for themselves if that is how they want to view the world! It's simply spewed out and left to rot in the frontal cortex of their developing mush. A great portion of us pass the same beliefs on to our children without ever allowing them the opportunity to form their own pure, original thoughts. We teach about war like it's normal, with a passive attitude that almost nonchalantly says, "It's okay that governments all over the world play on people's emotions and use their dedicated troops to murder and slaughter one another and innocent people, because, gosh dang it, that's just the way it is." Something about this method of thinking makes me want to scream, "It's not okay you fucking idiots!" But I digress.

I fear that we don't give our children the opportunity to form their own free thought. We form it for them through state-issued textbooks and state-regulated curricula and blatant propaganda. I see it firsthand every day, and it deeply saddens me. If we are to develop true leaders who represent all the good that humanity has to offer, then why do we deny our earthly future the opportunity to think for itself, truly? When you see children, what do you see? Do you see infinite possibility or booger-picking pains in the ass? If we can shed the entitlement we feel when we refer to ourselves as adults, then we would see that we are not above or below children. We are children still, only older and for some of us, wiser. So let's honor them by stepping outside of ourselves for a moment to really investigate if the public school system is a positive tool for growth or a tool for government control.

These little pieces of paper all over the floor from the hole puncher make me want to punch a hole in someone's fucking face.

3

DFH Syndrome

The custodial office is an interesting thing. Depending on the building you are in, it can be found in a variety of places. Some of those places include the basement, outside in a trailer, in an old classroom, in an old bathroom converted to a classroom converted to a custodial office, in a former administration office, in a former locker room, or maybe even in a closet big enough to fit a few grown men. (I've yet to see this, but I can almost guarantee it has been done.) Now, while most offices are made up of your standard necessities, some offices, such as mine, have their own special extras added on by the brilliant and creative minds that occupy it. Here is a mental image and a partial list:

A) a table
b) old chairs that teachers were throwing out. Custodians are in sync with the expression "One man's trash is another man's treasure" (as you will learn in the last inventory)
c) a couch or recliner, depending on the size of the space and the location (We have neither.)
d) a refrigerator, microwave, toaster oven, and a motherfucking coffeemaker
e) the boss's desk with a computer
f) random articles hung all over the walls and such: an old donkey piñata; a John Cena action figure; a papier-mâché pig with Ren

and Stimpy toys zip-tied to the top; a Christmas tree from the seventies; a wall full of pictures of women who were arrested for drunk driving and bribery; a sun piñata that makes you want to either drink a piña colada on a beach in Mexico or get stoned out of your mind, or both; a soccer trophy; a plaque with the words "The Kelsey DeWitt Theater Award" engraved on it (not sure who Kelsey was, but Kelsey, if you are reading this, thanks for the plaque, and I hope your acting career is taking off); a Boba Fett Star Wars mask complete with electronic voice; a sweet set of kitchen knives given as a present by the principal (don't worry, the kids can't reach them, and we only throw them after hours); and a ton of other random shit both work related and not.

I'll admit that our office is a bit more eclectic than most, but I am convinced that my boss is more of a genius than Good Will Hunting, only he has no clue that he is. I have a propensity for enjoying randomness, so it all works out just fine and in a way also leads me to my next point, but not really.

On the refrigerator in our office we have a few things hanging up. There are three comic strips, all dripping with sarcasm, that poke fun at either working for a living or the education system. There is also a sticker that says, "Water, Do Not Drink," and another bright-orange sticker that reads "Caution, Chemical Storage Area." Not sure how they got there, but the water sticker makes me chuckle, and the word *chemical* reminds me of the movie *Toxic Avenger* from the eighties. Downtime in this job mostly leads to nonsensical behavior, perhaps even immature and vulgar at times, and I'm pretty sure that's just the way most professional janitors like it. If they don't, then perhaps they are neither professional nor janitorial.

The most important and pertinent article hanging on our old, broken, leaking, crappy, hand-me-down refrigerator is the "Rules For Living" list. I guess you can say it is a simple list of twelve common courtesy rules. These are the type of rules that most adults learned way back when but then miraculously forgot to incorporate into their everyday lives as they got older. These twelve rules, if applied to the everyday routine, could probably change the future of the world, yet sadly, most people get what I would refer to as *dumb fuck-headedness*, or DFH syndrome, when it comes to executing them. Take a moment to read through them and ask yourself if you abide by these basic rules or you're a dumb fuck. And be honest. Don't worry. I will love you just the same: unconditionally.

RULES FOR LIVING

If you open it, close it.
If you turn it on, turn it off.
If you unlock it, lock it up.
If you break it, admit it.
If you can't fix it, call in someone who can.
If you borrow it, return it.
If you value it, take care of it.
If you make a mess, clean it up.
If you move it, put it back.
If it belongs to someone else, get permission to use it.
If you don't know how to operate it, leave it alone.
If it's none of your business, don't ask questions.

These rules seem so simple and logical and natural, yet they often go right out the window, floating away on a toxic breeze that smells of Glade air fresheners and polluted saltwater. Why is this?

It could be because most of us are raised in the public school environment, and we are taught that the only things that truly matter are your test scores and college and the prom and voting and sports and fitting in and doing what you're told without asking questions; all the other ethical and moral bullshit comes secondary. Children are taught to quickly pick something up and drop it just as fast; stand in line; keep that mouth shut. Do this, now do that; finish this, but start that before you finish this, then go back to that later; create, but only within the confines of the box we allow you to explore and create; go home and do homework because you haven't been through enough in the eight hours we've had you, and spending quality time with your family isn't going to pay the bills when you're older, so you might as well get used to it now anyway. Don't pick up that wrapper you just threw on the floor because someone else will get it later. Don't value the pencil you have because, hey, fuck it, you have a whole box of twenty, so who cares if you drop one and kick it to the side?

Who cares that there are children living in poverty who would find more value in that one pencil and piece of paper than they would in an ounce of gold? This is public school, man! Material excess and the blatant waste of goods are all part of the game. So go, go, go! Move, move, move! Hurry, hurry, hurry! But learn. Learn. Learn.

HE WHO HOLDS THE KEYS

Maybe I'm the prison guard walking the yard, locking the cell, casting a spell, wiping away freedom from the inside of a locker.

Maybe I ignore what it is I sweep off this floor, denying children more than what these fluorescent lights can illuminate.

Maybe I should bow my head and shut my mouth real tight, mop and dust and buff and shine and not put up a fight.

Maybe I'm the problem, and maybe we are lost, but maybe I can change the world with these daggers on my tongue.

4

The Fish Tank Effect

Let the wise guard their thoughts, which are difficult to perceive, extremely subtle, and wander at will.

—THE BUDDHA

We have six fish in a tank that sits in the wall right outside of the lunchroom. At one point, we had twelve. A fifth grade teacher by the name of Mike takes care of the tank, and I try to help out as often as possible. Over the last winter break, while everyone was out of school, I came in to work for the week, as custodians don't follow the same schedule as teachers and students. Instead of getting all three breaks (December, February, and March/April), we have to pick the one break we would like to take and then work the other two. (In New York, we get a weeklong break in February thanks to the oil embargo back in the seventies. Look into it when you get a chance.) The break that custodians choose is referred to by the administration as our holiday "option," but really, what option do we have besides having to work while the rest of the population is off enjoying Florida or playing at Lego Land or doing whatever the fuck it is that people with kids do on their time off. Serenity now, Tim.

When I got in to work on Monday morning, I went directly to the tank to feed those awe-inspiring creatures that breathe water and swim in their own urine. It was the month of December and being in the Northeast tends to bring with it some cold-ass weather. Coming up to the tank, I saw what can only be described as an aquatic genocide. There was death all over, bobbing and sinking. It was a terrible sight indeed and one that has permanently scarred me, almost like having Daddy issues, but more like fishy issues.

Like most human beings, I value life. *All* life. So seeing dead fish lying at the bottom of a rocky paradise made my heart sink. No pun intended. I quickly realized that we fucked up royally by forgetting to put the heater on in the tank before the long weekend, and seeing as how the boilers for the heat were not on in the building, six beautiful creatures froze to death. Yes, I am pretty sure it sucks to freeze to death no matter what species you are.

Among these fish was Marley, an incredible looking angel fish whom we had for only a short amount of time and whom I aptly named after the musical legend Bob Marley, because he had really long fins that looked like dreadlocks, and he seemed like a really chill fish (again, no pun intended), plus I guarantee he was the one rolling up the doobies for the other fish when everyone left the building for the night. I loved that fish, damn it. I really did. I watched him glide, move, and eat with intent. He had his own life and I Hans Soloed him, only he never made it back from the cryogenic chamber. I'm sorry, buddy.

Truthfully, I believe it is nearly impossible for human beings to grasp the concept of life and death. We try and we try, but in all reality, there are no answers to the why and how and where of it all. Some religions claim to know, yet every religious person I have ever met who has died has certainly not come back to tell me what happens after leaving this plane of existence, which serves to further strengthen my argument that it is *impossible* to know what happens when we die.

If we could figure out a way to appreciate that it just *is*, we would see that death is perfect and beautiful and not to be feared but embraced, just like birth.

The ego would lead many humans to believe that we are God's gift to the world and that we have "dominion" over the animals, until of course you go one-on-one with a lion, right? Then ask yourself who has dominion, you silly fucker.

I believe that within that fish tank there are more lessons to learn than any textbook could ever offer. There are lessons of wonder and curiosity and order and peace and love. Did the fish feel anything when they died? Did they suffer? How do they live day in and day out inside that small tank without ripping one another's heads off? Who is in charge? Is anybody? Do they talk about us in some weird fish language, cursing at us for knocking on the glass like the annoying shitheads we all tend to be? Do the kids in this school see that, wonder that, or *imagine* that? Teachers and students walk by three, four, five, six times a day and simply let the thought of a fish swimming around in a tank slip into their subconscious. It doesn't even cross their mind that there is a creature breathing water right next to them! It's just, I don't know, accepted.

For the most part, there is no amazement, no pondering, no *time* to do anything but look and move on. There is no sense of living in the present moment. No sense of cherishing the only real thing we have, which is the very breath we are taking right now. These children, *our* children, are part of the rat race before they even know what the rat race is. All eyes ahead, looking down the hallways that only lead to a lifetime of having your hard-earned money stolen by illegal taxes, banking on a made-up reality that doesn't exist anywhere else but in the future mind, and all the while never realizing the true potential behind the power of their present mind.

Here, they will never learn that the mind is both a gift and a curse. They will never learn that they are indeed beautiful fish in some weird reincarnated way, and that they have the chance to create their own environment with one another, peacefully. They are *life* and *love*. They are individuals with separate paths and callings but all part of the same tank. How can they blossom as individuals if they can't swim freely? How can we show them they are each unique and different, yet exactly the same? Breathe in, breathe out. Rest in peace, Marley. You were a dope fish.

From: Almeida, Timothy
Sent: Friday, November 14, 2014, 9:36 a.m.
To: Teachers
Subject: *Custodian Chronicles* Issue 1

THE CUSTODIAN CHRONICLES
Volume 1, November 2014

    I had a friend pass today. His name was Mambo Jackson. While his passing wasn't quite a surprise, it was certainly a sad good-bye and a tough lesson in learning how to let go of every passing moment. Some of you may have known him, and there is no doubt that you passed him in the hallways every day. He was the quiet type. Quiet, yet spunky. In order to get an idea of exactly who Mambo was, here is a list of three of his best attributes and the lessons to which those attributes contributed:

1. Listening

Mambo was like an old wise man on the hill. When you spoke to him, he would simply take it all in. Whether he reserved his judgments or simply had none, I will never know. What I do know is that any time I spoke, he listened, and after I was done sharing, I felt better. I learned that listening to friends trumps overbearing them with my endless list of complaints, any day of the year. It doesn't even matter that he spoke a different language than me. Empathy is universal.

2. Adaptation

At one point in time, Mambo was living in what many would consider a hostile environment. There were creatures surrounding him that were bigger, stronger, and meaner. For a while, his living arrangements were sketchy at best and near impossible at worst. (Picture Times Square back in the day, before Giuliani came in and made it all bland and touristy.) On a regular basis, Mambo had to scramble to survive, adapting to whatever was presented to him at the moment. He didn't think ahead, didn't look back. He just adjusted, accepted, and survived in the moment. And I am pretty sure he did it with grace and humility.

3. Fearlessness

Mambo had a condition. Most would refer to it as a deformity of sorts. Although he was never officially diagnosed, it seemed like he had either scoliosis or some type of degenerative spinal condition. Simply put, his body shape was weird. Almost like a boomerang or the curve on the top of a protractor. (Do they still make those things?) I know I'm only a custodian but from what I researched, my final diagnosis would be either tuberculosis or scoliosis. Still, Mambo was a stud. He exuded confidence and used his skills by making the best of himself. He didn't hide who he was. He lived life with a "love me for who I am, or leave me" type of attitude. No complaining about the cards he was dealt, no crying about his misfortune. He was fearless. Like Evil Knievel or Tony Hawk.

In all honesty, I have no qualms about the admission I am about to divulge to you, my fellow coworkers and human beings. I'm a thirty-six-year-old man with dreads, tattooed knuckles, and some serious street cred. (Actually, I grew up in Mineola and now live in Farmingdale, so my street cred is more like a mix of suburban wits and working-class grit.) But that does not change the fact that I shed a small tear over losing a fish that I have been feeding and watching almost every day for the last three years of my life. Mambo Jackson was a brilliant creature. He was quirky and unique and simply real. I can't allow my human entitlement to make me consider him "just a fish." Maybe to some he was, but for me, he was Mambo the king. I watched him get sick this week, than I watched him hide behind that fake log for a day, as if he knew it was his end, and then, it ended. Simple. No different than it does for us as people. So, let's celebrate being alive today, not because it's Friday, but because we are all traveling on this awesomely bizarre and inexplicable path together, and

we are lucky to be doing it. And last, let's pray that Mambo's soul doesn't reincarnate as a custodian. Until next time. Live, love, laugh, repeat.
Timothy Almeida
Master of the Custodial Arts
Est. 1978

Sometimes you have to play a long time to be able to play like yourself.

—MILES DAVIS

Although I have not learned how to care for my desk, at least I am prepared to pass this state test.

5

The Breakdown by the Numbers

And Other Ways to Escape the Torturous Sounds of a Mind Occupied by Mundane Bullshit

If you have ever seen the movie *Groundhog Day* with Bill Murray, you most likely remember the scene when Bill's character, Phil Connor, looks directly into the camera, and with a total look of defeat, exhaustion, and even anguish, says, "Hey, folks, it's Groundhog Day...again." The movie is about a news reporter who wakes up each morning only to find out that he is living the same exact day over and over again. Well, most days, being a custodian is just like that. Sound familiar?

As a custodian, I have to clean the same exact rooms, mop the same exact halls, wash the same exact shitty bathrooms, dust the same computers, scrub the same desktops, sweep the same goddamn floors that have so much garbage on them that you sometimes think students and teachers put it on the floor just to mess with you, and so on and so on. The other day, I found an entire sandwich, not one bite missing, just sitting on the floor. I shit you not. It was a Salami sandwich on white bread just laid out on the tile floor. Bleached, enriched white bread. Delicious.

I imagine that no matter what job you have, doing the same thing day in and day out is guaranteed to get tedious from time to time. Even if you absolutely love your job, you most likely still need to step away once in a while to decompress and learn how to find appreciation for it again. I'm pretty sure the main reason most of us grow to become gainfully employed in a nine to five is because we lacked the proper guidance to discover other options and automatically assumed we had to follow whatever societal standards were set before us. Grade school, college, more college, job, marriage, house, kids, more kids, retirement, another job, retirement again, travel, die. Sounds pretty bleak when presented that way, I know. To be honest, had I known then what I know now, I never would have stayed in school. Every crucial life lesson I have ever learned that carries any true value was most certainly not learned in a classroom. Some of my most valuable steps in personal growth have come from dealing with life on the outside of the systemic norms, going against the grain as opposed to going with it. That's not to say I haven't learned a great deal while carrying out my duty as a custodial ninja, because I certainly have. Let's chop it up and explore.

What I have learned inside these walls as a custodian is that the human mind has difficulty accepting reality, so we often wish for a different one without realizing that this action, the action of "wishing," is what makes us so miserable sometimes. We yearn for anything but the reality we live in. (This theme will recur in this book as I find it of the utmost importance to explore it thoroughly.)

There have been days when I look at the mess in front of me, and I almost get angry that I have to clean it up because I am looking for a different situation. Our favorite words are *I wish* and *if only*, and we fail to realize that this leads to suffering. As the brilliant psychologist and author Dr. Fred Hartman would say, "We want magic." It's not the actual moment we are living in that causes suffering. It's the constant craving for something else other than our present reality. This is Buddhism 101, and it's something I apply constantly to get through my work shift, because quite honestly, cleaning something until it is nice and shiny, only to come in the next day to see that it has been pissed on, spilled on, dropped on, or whatever, is pretty disheartening. So I simply just accept that it is what it is, and I repeat it over and over again, like Phil fucking Connor.

To give you an idea of what the job really entails, let me break it down for you. Most custodians refer to the area of the building that they clean as their "section." It includes every classroom, bathroom, office, etc. that is found within that designated part of the building. Usually, the people who work the day shift, which in my building is from 7:00 a.m. until 3:30 p.m., have a smaller area, a.k.a. section, than the ones who work the night shift, 3:00 p.m. to 11:30 p.m., because during the day the building is in use, so cleaning the classrooms is not an option since they are occupied, unless of course the kiddies decide to have a throwing up contest, which happens from time to time. That's when the day crew springs into action like fucking superheroes to rid the world of the villainous, vomitous state of disarray left behind by the evil children. I will attempt to get into more detail about the "day vs. night shift" theme in another chapter, or I may just save it for another book, or maybe not write about it at all. But for now, let's break this dirty bitch down:

TIM'S SECTIONAL BREAKDOWN BY THE NUMBERS

Classrooms: seventeen
Bathrooms: ten
Garbage cans: forty
Stairwells: three
Carpets: fourteen

WHAT I DO:
Every carpet gets vacuumed daily. Each floor is swept, or *dragged*, as we refer to it. Garbage cans get emptied. Stairwells get swept. Bathrooms get cleaned. Hallways get dragged as well. Dusting is done as needed, as well as cleaning desktops, blackboards, and sinks for the classrooms that have them. I change broken lightbulbs, replace toilet paper, paper towels, and hand soap, and I clean walls, windows, doorways, and pretty much anything else you can think of. Yeah, exciting stuff! I just clean, clean, clean. And clean. And clean.

LET'S DO SOME MATH, EVEN THOUGH I SUCK AT IT:

If I clean ten bathrooms a day—eighteen toilets and eight urinals—then by my calculation, that's fifty bathrooms a week, or ninety toilets and forty urinals weekly. There are approximately 180 days in a school year. So, if we multiply (one of the few things I actually did retain from public school) 180 x 10, we get (drum roll, please)...eighteen hundred! Yes, you read that correctly. Eighteen hundred! I clean the same ten bathrooms eighteen hundred times in one school year. Now if you really want to be impressed—or depressed, depending on how you look at it—that would mean those yellow urinals get scrubbed by my lucky hands 1,440 times per school year and the toilets a mere 3,240 times. Amen and hallelujah. I'll continue on and make it simple.

40 garbage cans/day = 200/week = 7,200 per year
17 Classrooms/day = 85/week = 3,060 per year

If this really whets your appetite, then by all means feel free to do the rest of the calculations for the carpets and stairwells. My only intention was to put into perspective just how much custodians actually have to do. It isn't easy, and it is very hard to get through it mentally some days. I just try to stay thankful and ignore the pungent smell of piss in my nostrils. Let's proceed.

It is important we bear in mind that I am but *one* custodian cleaning *one* area in *one* school inside of *one* district. There are nearly fourteen thousand districts in the United States. If we consider the fact that I *alone* throw out an estimated ten thousand bags of garbage per school year, then the only conclusion that we can draw from said fact is that it is insane.

It is sad, awful, perturbing, fucked-up, aggravating, and ridiculous, and it's my job. The guilt seeps through me knowing that I, as much as anyone else, am a plague on the environment. I am a parasite, a tapeworm in the earth's small intestine, a Venus flytrap to the ozone. As much as I try to save things, recycle things, reuse things, and be mindful, I know that I am still part of the problem due to my human conditioning. I am simply a thorn in the planet's side.

There is a cold truth that we must all accept: We are, without denial, destroying this planet every day. Every second of every day, someone somewhere is polluting, wasting, extracting, cutting down, pulling out, drilling in, picking up, dumping out, digging through, and using up. We are apathetic in our attempts to be thrifty, and we are poor examples for our children if we don't start to change our attitudes, our schedules, our routines, and our ways. In this institution the pencils hit the floor, the broom sweeps them up, and the students grab another one. This happens Monday through Friday, 180 days a year. Drop it, fuck it, grab another, waste it, throw it out, throw it out again, get me another one. Who cares, where does it all come from, where does it all go? We teach that "out of sight, out of mind" is the only way because the real value is not in the earth on which we live but in the dollar for which we die. Yes. That is it. The dollar needs to circulate, the bombs must drop, and the children must believe. Blessed universe, forgive us all.

I recently asked a group of fifth-grade students about where they thought all the garbage produced in this school actually went. I imagine it is not a detail thought about on a daily basis by most of us, and especially not by a group of ten-year-olds staring down the hallway with black-and-white circles where their pupils should be, hypnotized by the predetermined schedule that will control their lives from now until the day they walk across that stage, shake the principal's hand, and collect that diploma (which will certainly make its way into an old storage bin in Mom and Dad's attic). A few students said, "To a garbage disposal." Others said, "To a garbage dump."

In an attempt to peel the skull back from their brains a little more, with the hopes of unlocking some miracle realm inside their heads where they would suddenly have a collective epiphany about the impossible sustainability of the earth if we continue down this path of heedless, irrational, and blatant waste, I asked them where they thought it goes *after* the dump, to which one child responded, "The sky?" They simply had no idea of an answer, nor would they, and they seemed to quickly drift off into the murky waters of cafeteria sludge before returning to their regularly scheduled program of packaged deli meats, Minecraft, and fructose. I, on the other hand, began brainstorming on the words you are reading right now.

What...the...fuck? I can't understand how *one* floor, in *one* class-room, can get so disgustingly filthy inside of *one* day. Good god. It looks like an abortion gone severely wrong. What? You're only read-ing about it. I'm living it!

6

Who Needs Trees When You Can Have a Pencil Graveyard?

'm nearing one thousand, and I know because I counted. One thousand what, you might be wondering? Well, one thousand is the amount of pens and pencils that I have picked up off the floor while performing my janitorial duties. That isn't one thousand pencils and pens over a few years. That is one thousand pencils and pens inside of one year. That does not include the ones I happened to miss or the ones I admittedly was too lazy to pick up. It also does not include rulers, glue, glue sticks, notepads, erasers, colored pencils, highlighters, markers, and other classroom materials, which I happen to have a boatload of as well. The fact that I have collected this much is simply appalling, and it is our fault. The blame rests solely on the shoulders of every single adult that plays a part in influencing the life of a child. Any child. We are failing where it matters most and because of that, the planet suffers.

I write this with a tear in my eye, a fire in my belly, and love in my heart. Forget about the Common Core and state tests and guidelines and Regents boards and SATs and PSATs. Fuck textbooks and $x = y$. Screw the secretary of education who has never taught or spent a day in a classroom, and forget the state lunch program that requires any leftover food to be thrown out regardless of how many of us are willing to drive it to the neighborhood shelter. Who cares about the governor and his percentages and his toeing the party-line rhetoric and forget about all these local politicians who never take the time to visit a school unless it's election year. Let's cut through the belly fat and get to the truth. This *cannot* last.

I'll never miss the opportunity to pick up another pencil again, because my kids, our kids, deserve better than this. The amount of waste is incessant, despicable, and impossible to ignore. Like windup dolls being turned from our backsides by a cruel owner, we are set on autopilot to buy, buy, buy, discard, discard, discard, and destroy, destroy, destroy. One thousand pencils will turn into ten thousand pencils inside of a few years. Students will write about Earth Day and how important it is to care for our mother (only on Earth Day will they do this, even though they live on the earth for the other 364 days as well), not recognizing the irony with which they hold her in between their two fingers, scrawling, drawing, doodling, and taking tests, only to toss her to the curb once they've had their way with her.

In a given year, the United States cuts down anywhere from sixty thousand to eighty thousand trees to produce pencils. To put it in perspective, walk to the closest window, look outside, and count the amount of trees you see, than imagine that eighty thousand times over. Yeah, I know. It's baffling.

Are we so ingrained with our way of life inside these schools that we simply carry on without worrying about future consequence? Do we really believe it is normal for one student to use anywhere from fifty pencils or more in a single school year? And do we not see the hypocrisy in demanding students be respectful of teachers and classmates while we allow them to be totally unaware of the way in which they disrespect the very planet they live on? Wouldn't it make more sense to teach children how to value one pencil and make it last instead of requiring them to bring in a box of fifty at the beginning of the school year? Why not have them bring in just two pencils and provide them the opportunity to learn about appreciation, responsibility, and resourcefulness by being sure not to lose either of them? Then when they have used up those two pencils, they can bring in two more. Look how much we can teach them before we even make them open a book!

Some days, I wish I could come in and scream at the top of my lungs, "Stop what you are doing! You are fucking this all up! We are never going to make it like this!" I want to shake this building by its frame in order to jostle its systematic brain that thrives off insanity. Okay, fine, it's only a pencil, right? I shouldn't be that worked up over silly things like how many pencils we waste each year. There are bigger things going on in the world, like mass poverty and incarceration and war and pollution and...wait a minute. Now I see.

One thousand one, one thousand two...

> *Humankind has not woven the web of life. We are but one thread within it. Whatever we do to the web, we do to ourselves. All things are bound together. All things connect.*
>
> —Chief Seattle, 1854

7

Observations from a Broom Handle

What teachers HAVE to do:
Get students prepared for state-issued exams.
What SOME teachers WANT to do:
Get students prepared for real life.
What students HAVE to do:
Get prepared for state-issued exams.
What students WANT to do:
Run, play, explore, love and be loved, discover, evolve on their own and
at their own pace. Learn!
What teachers HAVE to do:
Follow a curriculum.
What SOME teachers WANT to do:
Run, play, explore, love and be loved, teach at their own pace, create
their own methods, and do away with mandatory testing. Learn!

8

The Kindergarten Nazi

A kindergarten class is sitting in the lunchroom, awaiting dismissal. The teacher stands in front of them, hovering, demanding silence. Two children continue to talk a few seconds too long. The teacher leans in close, her face a few inches away, and screams directly at one of the students: "Are you deaf?" Umm, no, she is five. I breathe deeply.

Imagine that is your child. Imagine shipping your child off to an old brick building every day to possibly be screamed at by a complete stranger for hours on end. Why do we do this? Furthermore, why do we do it every day with the assumption that it is healthy for our children? I distinctly remember being that five-year-old child once. To this day, I want to put those teachers in a triangle choke. (A submission hold practiced in the martial art of Brazilian jujitsu, where you render your opponent completely unconscious basically using only your two legs.) I want to sit those teachers down in a chair in front of the entire class and ask them if they remember what it's like to be five. I want to ask those teachers whether they see that their lack of patience and compassion stems from their own psychological pain, their own baggage. I want to tell the children who have also had to endure such a situation that it's okay to want to talk and be happy with your friends. It's okay to be five years old and to be daydreaming of unicorns and candy and of being a fucking princess in a castle made of ice. I want to hug those teachers and help them see what it is to find a true sense of patience, unwavering and sturdy. My brain goes berserk. Write...it...down.

I let the typical adult excuses to rationalize acting like a Nazi rattle around in my head, and I feel disconnected from the system, because I know it breeds authoritarian attitudes disguised as educated ones. Let's explore.

THE EXCUSES

1. These kids need to be taught how to listen!
2. If we don't teach them how to follow rules, then we'll have a world in chaos!
3. They need to learn how to respect adults!

THE JANITORIAL RESPONSE TO SUCH EXCUSES

1. **Children know how to listen.** What you want is for the child to hear you. If you want a child to hear you, or if you want anyone to hear you for that matter, speak *kindly* and patiently. Always. Every time. No excuses. Excuses are for children.
2. **Rules and laws are put into place because society fails as a whole to create solutions.** Although it is possible that the public school system creates generation after generation of subservient humans who are afraid of breaking "the rules," no matter how ridiculous those rules might be, I think it is about time we stepped away from the conveyor belt and allowed our children the opportunity to learn natural order and appreciation instead of manmade hierarchy.
3. **Those truly deserving of respect never demand it.** They live happily and humbly. They treat others with respect without expecting it back. As Maynard James Keenan, lead singer from the band TOOL, said, "Expectations are the road to hell." I'm pretty sure Buddha or some wise sage might have said that too, but Maynard is a badass and TOOL is one of the greatest bands ever. (FYI, Buddha was a badass too.) If anything, we should carry the

understanding that a child's mind is not developed enough to truly understand the idea behind respect, so maybe a steady and consistent stream of compassion will change that around. This seems to make sense to me, but really, who knows? End chapter.

The moral fiber that should be infused into the cellular structure of students is instead put to the wayside to meet the ludicrous demands of state mandates. Wherever you reside, whatever district your children attend, I can guarantee that the governor, secretary of education and many times even the board of education appointees will never have *your* child's best interest at heart. How can they when they don't clothe your child, feed your child, or live with *your* child?

9

Drug-Free Is the Way to Be, Unless We Diagnose You with ADD

Processed Sugar, High Fructose Corn Syrup, and Tasmanian Devils

There is a certain sound that resonates inside these walls. It is high-pitched screaming and screeching, like the dinosaurs in *Jurassic Park*. It's like that scene in *Kindergarten Cop* when the kids go ape shit. (Where the hell is Arnold Schwarzenegger when you need him?) Two hundred and fifty little voices chatting at once, making a diagnosis of schizophrenia seem more like a walk in the park. It is complete pandemonium, and it happens every day at the same time.

Ahh, you guessed it. It's the lunchroom: droves of elementary aged children crying, laughing, coughing, sneezing, puking, and crawling on the floor. Sugary drinks spilling, ice cream melting, and processed chips crunching. A fast-food bag that was most likely last night's dinner, covered in grease, being taken out of a Batman backpack so fragile young children can shovel down the fake meat and chemical fries without knowing that their internal organs cannot and will not be able to digest something so foreign to the body. It will just sit in their little intestines and do God knows what to their bodies for God knows how long. Sometimes a sandwich gets thrown or a kid purposefully takes his or her bagel with cream cheese and smears it across the floor, just for the fuck of it. This behavior is not gender specific. Boys and girls participate equally. Let's not forget the occasional lurching of vomit into the garbage pail, if they even make it that far, or if not, they usually just blow chunks right into their hands or on the table.

Of course we can't forget to add the lunch monitors into the mix, a.k.a. informal corrections officers, screaming at the screaming children, trying to keep the peace, as if these kids who are ingesting forty grams of sugar in one sip shouldn't be bouncing off the fucking walls like a meth addict looking for a fix.

It's hard for them to maintain order in such a frenzied environment. Instead of Tasers and batons, they are equipped with a whistle and clipboard; I imagine that part of the reason that some monitors tend to lose their cool so easily is because they are getting paid shitty money and really don't get much help. I also don't believe there is any formal training to be a lunch monitor. Hell, as far as I know, you don't even have to like kids. Maybe the interview process goes something like this:

Interviewer: Have you ever worked with children before?
Interviewee: No. Never.
Interviewer: Do you like children?
Interviewee: No.
Interviewer: Hmm, I see. Well, seems to me you're perfect for this job. You start Monday!

Welcome to the cafeteria, my friends! Where nutrition isn't even a passing thought, and children shove food down their throat faster than a hooker in the South Bronx takes a you-know-what in her you-know-where. First of all, who the fuck came up with the bright idea to let kids drink milk and eat pizza at the same time! It's a recipe for disaster.

Here ya go, youngsters! Eat this slice of pizza that was made with an obscenely acidic sauce that most likely came out of a can or was made from chemically treated tomatoes (so in all reality it probably contains no nutritional qualities) and don't worry about what it does to your body. (Often, tomatoes are gassed with the plant hormone ethylene to ripen them, or injected with red dye to make them look more appealing, or both of these combined. Further, some studies show that there are chemicals in the aluminum can that make their way into that wonderful sauce, which then makes its way into the body.)

And never mind all that genetically modified bread and cheese that's going to hit your stomach like a fucking brick falling from the top of a construction site. Just wash it down with this hormone-infested milk. It's the same milk that a poor cow was tortured into producing by way of artificial insemination, after which they had to gestate for ten months to prepare for the calf they will give birth to and simultaneously have taken away on the same day. They then got milked until their udders become so infected that they live every day of their life in agony, contract the disease mastitis (which by the way, often makes its way into the milk everyone is drinking) and are then sent to slaughter by their fourth or fifth birthday, even though cows have an average life span of twenty years. And as if that isn't awful enough, after you drink this milk, young boy or girl, run around outside for a few short minutes, or inside, depending on the weather, and try your very best not to puke your guts up.

This is not a fictional scenario I have conjured up to amuse you, although when I read it back, I must admit it is pretty entertaining. This is a reality that *our* children endure every day, and it's unfair to them and their future.

One of the hardest things about being a custodian is sitting and observing the behaviors that you know will be detrimental to our future as a society—to not only have to accept the amount of waste public schools produce, but to have to deal with cleaning it up. The lunchroom is certainly no exception to this truth. Children are shuffled in, given an unfair amount of time in which to eat (which might be better for some kids, considering the "food" they are given), and then shuffled out to enjoy a half hour to do what kids are meant to do: run around and play! The idea of actually taking your time and being thankful for what you are eating without having to worry about finishing before you even start is nonexistent. It is literally a prison setting.

Children come in single file, sit, are told to be quiet over and over again, ingest, for the most part, awful and unhealthful food, and then get pushed out in order for the next shift to make its way in. Whatever food they don't eat, they are told to throw out. "Fuck it! Throw it out! Who cares? Better yet, just throw it on the floor. One day, when you're older, perhaps you'll see the value in the necessities for survival, but until then…" You get my point.

While so many parents I know are awakening more every day to how detrimental the standard American diet (SAD) is to their children's health, it is quite surprising to see that while their kids are in school, they are consistently exposed to so many unhealthy options. Yes, kids should be able to enjoy some sweets from time to time. Hell, I am a self-proclaimed chochoholic! But kids should not be drinking high fructose corn syrup like it's water and should certainly not be eating cupcakes at nine o'clock in the goddamn morning. Let's think about this madness!

A child who weighs sixty pounds ingests fifty grams of sugar. That is nearly one gram of sugar per pound of body weight. That child is then asked to not only sit still but to also concentrate on something that might not interest him/her at all! If that child fails to do so often enough, then there is a good chance that his/her parents will be brought in to the school psychologist and force-fed information and misinformation about attention deficit disorder, more commonly known as ADD (a condition that seems to have been exacerbated by pharmaceutical companies in order to inundate the masses and make a profit off Ritalin and Prozac sales), and then possibly their children will be placed on a prescription medication to deal with their "behavior issues," which most likely stems from a piss-poor diet and a lack of interest in dividing fractions.

If my memory serves me correctly, there was no clinical diagnosis for ADD when I was a child. Notice I said "if" my memory serves me. I'll admit that sometimes it serves me such an overabundant stream of words and thoughts that if I were to articulate those words and thoughts, I would certainly be tied down on a laboratory table, dissected, and found to be too strange and confused to draw a conclusion. That is neither here nor there, nor there, nor there, nor here! See what I mean?

We are literally creating a nation of zombies dependent on pills. For example, we all know a friend, family member, or coworker who takes something for either anxiety or depression. Hell, I used to sniff Xanax just for fun! (Not recommended, by the way. It is a terrible, terrible idea.) It makes perfect sense for certain pharmaceutical companies to be in bed with the US Department of Education, and it sure as fuck makes sense for them to want our children to never have the chance to learn the inner workings of their own minds and instead be dependent on pills that dull the senses and literally change the brain chemistry. Yes, yes, the almighty dollar comes knocking again. Best believe it is hard at work trying to medicate and sedate our little gems. It's madness, I tell ya! Madness! Am I paranoid? I don't think so. I am considering *all* possibilities, and that is a scary yet liberating thing to do. So go ahead and get to it!

It is obvious to see that the human mind is naturally distracted. It is a constant stream of electronic impulses firing from neuron to neuron, so the idea of impulsively labeling a child with ADD is preposterous. Not every child is meant to sit in a classroom and certainly not every child has the personality type to endure the trials of the public school system. What the "system" does is automatically assume that the individual can conform to the herd, and that is exactly why the system is broken and was never meant to work.

There is no capital to be gained for corporations, which is exactly what the public school system has become, if we start to mold children into freethinking individuals. Big Pharma, Big Agro, Big Brother—all are snakes in the grass, stalking our kiddies, slithering under the blackboard, fangs out, dollar signs in the eyes. Just to refresh, remember what was said earlier:

In our dream we have limitless resources, and the people yield themselves with perfect docility to our molding hand...

I guess dreams do come true.

PS—While I am consciously aware of the nonhealth benefits of pizza, I still eat it. The difference is, I *know* that I am eating it, and I only do so on occasion. Also, if you live in New York and don't eat pizza once in a while, then you should seriously reconsider your reasons for staying here or maybe just end your miserable existence now. I'm kidding. Eat some pizza first, than hang yourself. Seriously though, I struggle daily with the whole "eat it, don't eat it" theme. Save the animals! Where does this food come from? Am I a hypocrite? Well, I suppose I am, but I try my best not to be. Word up.

The copy of *People* magazine in the teachers' lounge just made my IQ drop by thirty points. I literally feel dumber. Yes, my point exactly. FYI, I only read it 'cause I needed something to entertain me while I took a smash.

10

Teacher, dear teacher, do you not give a damn? Every single day you put half a cup of coffee upside down in your garbage can.
You tell me you're sorry but fail to think, just a few steps farther and you could have poured it in the sink.
I do not get mad, for I am used to the routine, although I often wonder if you are the same at home, or is your house superbly clean?
I understand that all day you are stuck inside this class and that when the weather gets warm, your room smells like sweaty ass. And even though it's a fire hazard to hang things on that glass...you've made it quite clear that you will ignore any such requests and hang that crappy poster anyway.
Teacher, dear teacher, I will now vacuum your rug and ponder my existence as a measly little bug.

For any teachers reading this, please feel free to frame it and put it on your desk. Love you.

~GOOD TIM HUNTING~

50

11

I Pledge Allegiance to...Johnny from The Karate Kid?

Blind Nationalism and Patriotic Nonsense

At the age of five, when children are in kindergarten, they are required to remember and recite the Pledge of Allegiance. Before we explore this unquestioned cultural norm, let us first forget everything we have ever been told and open our minds. Forget all the stars and stripes, the bombs bursting in the air, and the Uncle Sam lingo that convinces young men and women to enlist so some of them can guard poppy fields in Afghanistan so the CIA can peddle their heroin back and forth. For starters, the word *allegiance* needs to be explored and is not something we ought to overlook. As defined in the Merriam-Webster dictionary, allegiance means

- the obligation of a feudal vassal to his liege lord; and
- the fidelity *owed* by a *subject* or citizen to a sovereign or government.

Fidelity by its own definition means the faithfulness and loyalty a person continually demonstrates to a cause or belief. Let's really, really, *really* think about this for a moment. How is it realistic or even remotely logical for us to ask a five-year-old child to pledge an allegiance and place a belief in something they are unable to critically explore and cannot possibly understand at all? Why do we ignore the unhealthy possibilities associated with this exercise of pledging? Who is it exactly that our children are pledging to? The flag? The government? The president? The people? A community? The military? America? Walmart? Toys"R"Us? Sponge Bob Square Pants? Black Michael? Light-skinned Michael? White Michael? Transparent Michael? Hess gasoline? The guy who played Johnny in *The Karate Kid*?

Sounds preposterous right? That's because it is! For all they know, it could be any combination of the above list, and it still wouldn't make an ounce of difference. We are not instilling the honorable trait of loyalty in them. We are programming allegiance to a concept we believe to be freedom. We are uploading a viewpoint and letting it run wild.

I mean this from the center of my precious heart. Our children could be pledging allegiance to a scary-looking clown taking a shit while reading a newspaper and listening to the soundtrack from *Footloose* (hell yes, Kevin Bacon, that last dance scene is amazing!), and they still wouldn't know the difference. I say this because when a child says the pledge every day, five days a week, 180 days a year, there is not one iota of consciousness present as they recite those words. They go on autopilot every single time. They are taught only the *words*, empty of the actual meaning behind those words.

Anyone who has ever attended public school was also taught those words, and most of us continue to blindly recite them as adults and simply chalk it up to being "proud" of our country. We have been made to believe that we are the greatest country in the world before we even have a chance to actually go to another country and decide for ourselves! It's quite fascinating to me.

Are we asking or demanding unwavering loyalty in the face of the flag or in the face of the government? At the very least, we have to objectively explore the idea of indoctrination taking place inside these public school walls. Why? Because in order for us to have a decent shot at progress and evolution, in order for us to truly mold the next generation into peaceful, intelligent, open-minded individuals, we must first be able to critically distinguish between patriotism and loyalty, pride and humility, freedom and slavery. As I've already touched on before, I do not believe it is fair of us as adults to instill *our* beliefs in children. It is not right of us to demand a loyalty to something as complex as a country and all it entails.

Pride is a dangerous and overbearing endeavor. We are all probably familiar with the phrase "The lord loves a humble heart," and although humility is one of the most difficult characteristics for the human ego to grasp, it is not beyond our reach to start to instill this desirable attribute into the everyday lives of our children. By having students commit to a mantra day in and day out, we are literally programming their brains to function in a specific and set way. When a mantra is performed repeatedly over an extended period of time, be it a Buddhist chant, a Catholic prayer, a Muslim salat or a national anthem, the person who is uttering that specific phrase is creating neurons and pathways in the brain that record and store that information. (Don't ask me how I know this, I'm just a custodian, for Christ's sake.) Logic dictates to me that that information is then processed by the unconscious mind, the opposite of awake, and then re-formed as a *belief*, which in the case of the pledge, leads most of the American population to think we are the sole custodians of the earth and the only ones entitled to do whatever the fuck we want with it. This is a belief that starts when we can barely wipe our own asses and lasts until we are old geezers, yet again unable to wipe our own asses and set in our ways, shackled to our personal belief system.

What is it about our insistence on believing in things? Why are we so afraid to say, "I don't know?" Human beings hang on to convictions like drunks hang on to the straps on the seven train, swaying and tilting, cursing and bleary-eyed, until they are so enraptured with their *idea of the truth* that the rest of the world becomes a misconception to them, a computer virus that is trying to attack what they know to be true, until all other viewpoints are hogwash, poppycock (that word is hilarious), and rubbish. It's what happened to us as kids, programmed to a certain faith, language, belief system, thought pattern, circuit board; and it makes us close-minded, arrogant pricks as adults. I think it's time to start pledging allegiance to humanity, the earth, the universe, and the only *truth*, that almighty and powerful word: LOVE.

SOMETHING TO PONDER:

Are you, as an adult, happy with the actions of your president(s), government(s), school system, local politicians, environmental services, state departments, and so on and so forth? Are you satisfied with having federal and state tax taken out of every single check you work for? Are you confident that money is going toward creating a better world for your children and grandchildren? Are you truly, *truly* satisfied with the direction in which we are moving, or not moving, depending on how you view it? Do you believe that war creates peace? Do you believe peace is realistic? Are we all one? Do our children know that to some people, namely the major corporations that control the wealth and the military industrial complex, that they are considered collateral damage? Do we know? Do we want younger generations living check to check like so many do now? Are you aware that it will most likely mean living in poverty in another twenty years? Have you ever stopped long enough to see who you truly are? Have any of us?

Note: All accounts show that Francis Bellamy wrote the pledge in August of 1892. He was a Christian Socialist, which is kind of an oxymoron in itself.

There are pamphlets in the main office titled "Caring for Our American Flag." Given the fact that hundreds of thousands of people live homeless in this country and our oceans are filled with garbage, maybe it's about time we changed that pamphlet title to "Caring for the Earth and All of Its Inhabitants." Now that's something our kids should be forced to read about. Betsy Ross. Fucking hilarious.

12

Checkmate

The two enemies of human happiness are pain and boredom.

—Arthur Schopenhauer

Wednesday, November 19, 2014
Sweep classrooms. √
Empty garbage. √
Clean desktops. √
Scrub sinks. √
Sweep hallway. √
Vacuum. √
Clean bathrooms. √
Replace broken chair. √
Fifty push-ups. √
Put garbage in shed. √
Take contractual break. √
Call Dad about Mom's sixty-fifth birthday party. √
Go back to work. √
Sweep classrooms. √
Empty garbage. √
Vacuum. √

Clean kindergarten tables. √
Clean bathrooms. √
Sweep hallway. √
Fifty push-ups. √
Sweep staircases. √
Dust. √
Feed fish. √
Lock shed. √
Shut off lights. √
Secure building. √
Go home. √
Repeat tomorrow. Fuck.

13

Green Grass, White Picket Fences, Drugs, Slingshots, and Boredom

Life is one big road with lots of signs, so when you riding through the ruts don't you complicate your mind. Flee from hate, mischief and jealousy. Don't bury your thoughts, put your vision to reality...

—Robert Nesta Marley

In 2006, I was arrested and subsequently convicted for driving while intoxicated. To be boldly honest, I probably could have and should have been arrested for the same crime on any given night starting from the age of eighteen, when I first got my driver's license. My reasons for telling you this are relevant to this book. First, allow me to bore you to sleep with a brief synopsis of my upbringing.

I grew up in a working-class town located in central Nassau County, Long Island, New York. The community was a mix of middle class and lower-middle class with some living poor, and no one that I knew of living wealthy. Growing up, I was lucky enough to have been surrounded by a variety of cultures. A few generations of Portuguese immigrants heavily populated my town and many bore children whom I am proud to have grown up with. It's because of this that I can, to this day, tell you to fuck off in the Portuguese language if need be, and if it is warranted, I can apologize in Portuguese as well. There was also an amazing mix of black, white, and Latino, and looking back now as a grown man, it is apparent to me how this particular setting has shaped my perspective on life. We are who we were around the people that we met in the past, only now.

If you decided to partake in the daunting and horrendous task of looking up statistics for Nassau County you would see that we have a shit ton of people crammed into a relatively small geographic area. I am not exaggerating when I say that there are literally millions of people hustling and bustling to and fro every day, which leads to awful, aggravating traffic and also makes everything so damn expensive, just like California, only it snows here and gets colder than a witch's teat during the winter months. Normally, the air is thick with stress and anxiety, and road rage is something that people practice day in and day out.

Around 1947, the first suburban community, Levittown, was built here. It is interesting to note that this development was strictly intended for white people only. A 2000 census survey showed that 94 percent of this area is still Caucasian. This serves as a grim reminder of how far we have yet to actually come in terms of our acceptance of humanity as *one* unit. Segregation and systemic racism are at the foundation of our country, and education on these issues is widely neglected inside the public school classroom, and in my opinion, neglected on purpose. The truth is often painful but liberating, and if we took the time to inform students about the harsh realities of our past, I imagine we would start to make some progress toward true equality.

Since the forties, a lot of the real estate development in these parts has grown to look the same. House, house, house, mall, house, house, mini-mall, highway, house, house, another freakin' mall, a highway leading into the mall! It's pretty much like that over and over again. If you head east, you will cross over into what is called Suffolk County. Suffolk boasts a much roomier layout. There is a huge farming community, and it consists of beautiful landscapes, albeit very flat ones as there are no mountains here and very little elevation, and there are lots of hidden treasures to visit. Some say it's just a matter of time before Suffolk County becomes one huge development like Nassau, but I'd like to think that the generations to come will see how important it is to preserve the "East End." I can only hope and pray that as they get older, they will be advocates for maintaining its beauty and charm.

Being that we are on an island, you hit water any way you go. North, south, east, and west, it doesn't matter. There is salt water on all four sides. Truthfully, the summers are what we live for. Memorial Day weekend somewhat resembles an ancient goddess giving birth to an angel wearing a crown made of surf wax, suntan lotion, and cold beer, metaphorically speaking. The beaches are beautiful, even though most people abuse them and destroy them, and I am of the belief that if summer didn't exist, then every single one of us would leave this overpriced shithole and head for the hills. I guess we stay because it's what we know and what we convince ourselves we love, and part of me does love it in some peculiar, hate-filled way.

I grew up on the same block as the hospital I was born in. So did my brother and sister. My father was a general contractor in the earlier part of my life, and after he closed his business, he moved on to become a superintendent of buildings and grounds in—you guessed it—the public school system! My mother was a hairdresser and stay-at-home mom, and later became a physical therapy assistant.

My elementary school was four blocks from my house, and I am pretty sure that as soon as I was old enough to walk there, I did. In the eighties, we lived in a society that seemed a hell of a lot less paranoid than it is today. Back in those days, if a parent let their nine-year-old kid walk to school they didn't have to worry about Child Protective Services coming to their front door and asking questions. We were smart enough to know not to walk up to a plain white van with tinted windows and not to take candy from a stranger, unless it was Halloween. (Then we took candy from as many strangers as possible.) Yeah, I know. The irony is baffling at times.

I often wonder if the world is any more or less dangerous than it always has been. History is riddled with stories of different tribes and militaries and cultures murdering one another by the millions for land, gold and riches, and yet we seem to be convinced that the world is more perilous now than ever before. I guess that's why we are so fortunate to have our government taking care of us and protecting us from the evil-doers! (Sarcasm, duly noted.) Good and evil have always operated the same. Some call them God and the devil or angels and demons; others call them dark and light. Me, I just call it humanity. Good old psychotic humanity.

Most elementary schools in this region consist of kindergarten through the fifth grade. Middle school is sixth through eighth, and high school is grades nine through twelve. From what I remember of my earlier years, I was an excellent student and energetic to a fault. I was involved in tons of sports and always had a deep love for music. I was kind and respectful and generous and outgoing. I was also a mama's boy and, come to think of it, a bit of a pussy in some ways. I didn't like physical confrontation, and seeing other kids get into playground scuffles gave me anxiety. I tried to avoid fights but certainly had my fair share of playground scraps. I definitely got my ass whupped on more than a few occasions, that's for damn sure.

While my love for sports and music remain with me today, it was in the eighth grade that my academics started to change. In hindsight, I can say with assurance that I began to grow bored of the general routines associated with suburban living. Puberty was kicking in, and my electrically charged, chemically juiced brain started to become restless and out of control, almost like the scenes on those *Girls Gone Wild* tapes from back in the day, but without the tits and ass and creepy camera guy. I was simply becoming anxious and mischievous, as were the friends and acquaintances I ran with. Around this time I began to view my community differently. It felt like my life was turning into a made-for-TV movie. The idea of school started to become a meaningless premise to me—pointless and mundane—so I searched for ways to get away from the same schools, same class subjects and vacation breaks every year, same smells, same faces, same parks, and same existence. I was searching outwardly, void of all introspection, and I fear now that we are teaching our children to do the same. It isn't our present situation that determines our happiness. It is our full acceptance of the present situation that ultimately leads to peace.

I was twelve years old the first time I smoked a cigarette. It was behind the garage of the auxiliary police station, which was located adjacent to the middle school I attended. To give you a better idea of the land layout, I've included a brilliant map for you to reference. Keep in mind that I have meticulously worked on this day and night to provide you with the finest detail and imagery imaginable.

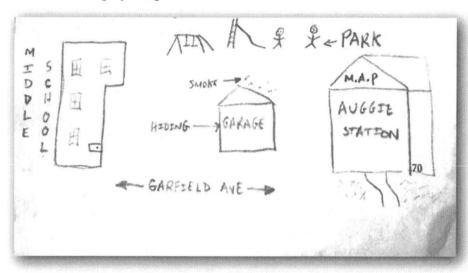

Joining me in this nicotine-filled soiree (which took place during the daytime, so it technically couldn't be considered a soiree) were two of my friends, whose names I shall conceal because I am presently still friends with them, and I don't want my mother blaming them for what was the beginning of a fairly consistent eighteen-year stretch of partying and debauchery. In retrospect, making the decision to smoke my first bogie (suburban street slang for cigarette) behind an auggie (more suburban street slang for auxiliary) police station was an obvious precursor of things to come. I can say with all sincerity that from this moment on, I would spend a lot of my days and nights acting as an emotionally unconscious, shitty kid. Not necessarily a bad kid, but a shitty one in terms of how I treated myself and the loyalty I showed to others. The shittiest thing about my shittiness was that I was really good at presenting myself to teachers, parents, coaches, and the like and convincing them I wasn't shitty, but I was in many ways a lost soul. I was an unbalanced creature. This is how many of our youth feel today. I can guarantee it.

My friends and I loved hanging out, and we loved disturbing the peace. I mean we seriously enjoyed fucking things up. No amount of Ritalin or Prozac would have curbed our enthusiasm to ride around town, steal people's newspaper money, destroy property, break into buildings, get in fights, propel objects at moving cars, and basically live as menacing a reality as we could. We were raging against something stagnant and trivial, awkward and anxiety-ridden. It's almost like school became a place for us to meet up, between getting messed up and creating chaos, like a teenage day-care center for delinquents.

Back then, most parents would let their kids go off and do their own thing so long as they were back for dinner at six o'clock. This would leave parents unaware of the trouble their kids were causing, and really speaks volumes about how selfish kids can be when it comes to violating the trust of another human being. Now I'm not saying *all* kids were troublemakers, but my crew certainly was. We were a bunch of BMX-bike–riding bandits, slingshots and all. Part of me still finds it hilarious, our shenanigans, but the grown-up in me is fully aware of the negative karmic energy I have bestowed on myself, even to this day.

By the time I was entering ninth grade, I got high for the first time. Instead of taking my chances behind a semiformal police station, we decided to be more discreet, so we went behind the bushes of my elementary school. I remember it clearly to this day. My buddy rolled a joint of the dirtiest, shittiest, seediest marijuana that the earth had ever produced up to that point. It popped and hissed as we dragged on it, and the conversation revolved around whether or not we would actually feel the high. Apparently the first time some people indulge in the sweet cheeba smoke, they don't respond to it. In essence, they feel no influential effects whatsoever. Well, not for me! My first time, I got stoned to the beejeebers and, as I'm sure you can guess, I loved it. At the time, I wasn't quite sure why I took to it with such grand enthusiasm. If we separated the reasons into different categories we could probably label them as part rebelliousness, part escapism, and part existential stagnation. Either way, I developed a long-term and eventually unhealthy relationship with pot. We actually broke up for a while, pot and I, but we have reunited again in my thirties and occasionally enjoy a night together. It is a much more balanced and positive relationship than it was back then, which just goes to show that *all* types of relationships have room for maturity and newfound health. It really is *all* a matter of the mind!

There is something fascinating about the idea of me trying drugs for the first time on the very properties that were supposed to keep me away from such endeavors. After smoking that first joint, we immediately walked about a half mile to the high school, where we continued to get baked with some other friends. We were twelve and thirteen years old, enjoying our "free" time hanging out at the one place we never wanted to be. I imagine if the curriculum had been changed to blunt rolling and bong smoking then much of our thirst for knowledge would have been restored. Instead, every year we endured the four core subjects—math, science, English, and social studies—along with a few electives, and just kinda made our way through.

For me, knowledge and education are not necessarily synonymous. The idea of education, in which people attend some sort of institution to learn a set curriculum, carries certain restrictions that cannot be bent. For example, when we sit in a class and listen to a teacher, the learning can only go as far as that instructor will allow. Sometimes, if a student presents a question that the teacher is unable to answer or does not have the time to answer, the student is then left to either

1. research that answer on his/her own time, or
2. forget the question in order to "keep up" with the rest of the class.

Knowledge, both universal and self, has no schedule of when it needs to be learned. It is quite remarkable to observe the way in which we choose to live, measuring our existence by the rolling numbers and ticking seconds associated with a manmade idea such as time. Time is the only thing we actually do have. It is infinite and invisible. If this is true, then why do we stress over running out of it, or not being on *time*? We are always on time, because time is always on.

Public schools fail to grasp this concept because the goal of childhood education is to get students prepared for the "real world," where the dollar is the boss and the clock is the foreman. Sadly, our real world is really fucked-up and dysfunctional. Ninety-nine percent of us do what we have to do to survive, with some moments of real happiness, greater moments of semihappiness, and most moments in stress and disarray. What do we have to do to turn this around? This I ponder from the top of my mop. Now, let's get back to the drugs!

Okay, kids, you've heard it, you've learned it, and you've most likely believed it at some point, or maybe you still do. "Marijuana is the gateway drug! If you smoke pot, you will turn into a heroin addict who turns tricks on the turnpike and steals from old ladies coming out of church!"

While some of you may end up doing that, it is certainly not related to smoking pot. It is related, again, to self-understanding. As is my mantra, all things are of the mind, and from both personal experience and outward observation, if there is one drug that will completely make you lose your mind and transform you into the fucking devil on steroids it is certainly not "the pot." No, no, no. The one substance that will cause your mind to completely shut down and allow you to do things you never would do while sober, is, strangely, the most socially accepted: alcohol. As anyone who has ever had a hangover will tell you, alcohol can be quite an evil matter, and if it is not handled with caution, well, I'm sure you know how that goes. "Ugh, what happened? Where am I? Did we have sex? What the fuck is that smell? I did? I lit what on fire? Shit, dude, again? My bad." Let us continue.

Most of us are familiar with that poisonous liquid substance that we dilute with other liquids because, let's face it, if we didn't, we would most likely die from ingesting it. Beer, wine, whiskey, gin, Zima, Boone's, motherfucking Colt 45 (bless you, Billy Dee Williams!), is all diluted. The reason we don't drink pure alcohol is that it would kill us, but hey, mix that shit up with something, and we are game.

This is a known fact that we also do not present to students. Instead, we teach them to "drink responsibly" when the very idea of drinking anything carries with it an air of irresponsibility. For instance, if an adult has one drink, it is recommended that he or she does not drive for at least an hour. Now what happens if there is an emergency within that hour? What happens if the babysitter calls because one of the kids cut a finger off with a butter knife? If we are unable to drive because we decided to indulge in a cocktail, are we being irresponsible, or did we just drink responsibly, neglecting all other responsibilities?

As I've grown older, I have found myself in an interesting place with alcohol. For starters, I no longer have the urge to drink to the point of blacking out, and I have taught myself how to drink a glass of wine without feeling the need to drink the entire bottle. In reality it is absolutely irresponsible for us to put a poisonous substance in our bodies and then rationalize it by saying that it's okay to drink, but not too much, and never when driving. This logic is flawed, and a huge part of the reason we have an epidemic of alcohol-related deaths, injuries, and the like in this country. We fail to learn the true tenets of self-control and discipline, and in doing so we doubly fail by not teaching our kids the same. We expect them, by the age of twenty-one, to be able to put a toxic substance in their bodies, one that immediately affects the brain and motor functions, and to then be able to make smart decisions, display lucid thinking, and not act like assholes.

During my high school experience, alcohol was rampant. I assure you that in this day and age, any young adult who attends public school will certainly be exposed to drugs. This is a fact that makes us seem content to settle for a presentation in the gymnasium once a year that tells students, "Don't do drugs" or "Hugs, not drugs." It's the type of presentation where someone who was a victim of drunk driving comes in and tells his or her story two days before the big homecoming game, or an old lady tries to connect with fifth graders and warn them about the dangers of drugs right before the school nurse gives 20 percent of them their daily dose of meds to curb their, you guessed it, attention deficit disorder, or as I like to refer to ADD, *amassing dollars daily*.

Aside from alcohol, the hypocrisy behind the entire "war on drugs"—and the way in which is presented in schools—makes my fucking skin crawl. It's a sham, and if you decide to take the time to research its history, you will see that its intentions were strictly politically and racially motivated. Like Joe Rogan, sports commentator, comedian, and TV personality always says, "It's a war on *some* drugs." Best believe the big pharmaceutical companies who are in bed with the federal government will always find a way to peddle their shit to the youth. Get them hooked young enough, and they'll never know the difference. Alcohol will always be pushed into the forefront as a cultural norm. To call it anything less than taboo in this society is complete fuckubbish. (See what I just did there? I combined the words fuck and rubbish. Use it at will. You're welcome.)

We cannot continue to participate in our cultural habit of presenting drugs as separate entities from alcohol. When people say drugs *and* alcohol, shouldn't they really just say drugs? Alcohol is a drug, as is Zoloft, Xanax, coffee, and Robitussin, which by the way, we used to drink bottles of in high school just to get banged up. We called it "Robo'ing." It can best be described as being drunk but with a tinge of an acid high mixed in. Coherent yet not, maybe hallucinating, maybe not. Yep, good times. Tylenol, Advil, Nyquil, Vicodin, Percocet, Viagra, Naproxen, Azithromycin, Lexapro, and even Amoxicillin. These are all drugs and all readily available at your neighborhood pharmacy. So why don't we include these in our war on drugs? Why don't we tell students that these are "gateway" drugs and should be avoided at all costs? Who decides what products are deemed acceptable and safe? This one is okay, but not that one. Take the red pill but never the blue one (unless you're having erectile dysfunction). Take a sleeping pill that was made in a laboratory to get a good night's rest, but never take a toke of the green plant that *grows out of the earth*. I know you see where I am going with this. Who makes the rules? And do you agree with them? I sure don't. I say change your perception, change your world, and then you will see through the hex.

We drank a ton of booze in my neighborhood. We often drank at school. Sometimes we even drank before and after school. The only exception to the rule for me was during wrestling seasons, when I would cut it all out and focus on training and competing. But I smoked cigarettes steadily until my senior year and then became an on-again, off-again smoker for the next seven or eight years. My high school even had a smoking lounge! My, how times have changed, and in this case certainly for the better.

What public school never taught me about is the most important subject of my life: *me*. It never gave me the tools to succeed within. Its focus on making sure kids go to college so they have the skills to be "competitive in a global market" is absolutely ludicrous and a downright lie. If that is really the case, then why does it cost $40 gazillion to go to college? Why wouldn't our elected leaders want us to get an affordable—or dare I say *free*—education? The answer is simple. It's because public school, like all other bureaucratic institutions, is big business. While this is an unfortunate truth, I believe that the people are starting to awaken to this, and I have no reservations about what our future holds in terms of fighting for fair and equal treatment for our respective communities.

Up to the point of my arrest, I lived a life of imbalance with pitfalls and triumphs. I would drink and do drugs, lots of cocaine, a boatload of Ecstasy, prescription pills, hallucinogens, whatever, and I would emotionally hit rock bottom. I would then fight my way back to the top, stay sober for extended periods of time, stay wasted again for a longer period of time, try to go to programs such as Narcotics Anonymous (I actually saw one of my high school teachers at one of those meetings once!), attend AA meetings here and there, feel good about myself, then feel not so good, drink, do drugs, repeat. I was resentful about who knows what, and I despised the idea of rules and laws and conforming. I still do now, only that resentment has faded, and instead my nonconformity comes from a place of love and the desire to evolve, and not from a place of hate. The meetings I went to made me feel like I was an eternal screw-up, as if there was no hope for me because I was powerless over drugs, powerless over my own self—like there was something chemically wrong with my brain that could not be fixed with proper exercise and nutrition. It made me feel utter despair—as if life was a pointless joke. I didn't want to believe that I could "never have a drink again" because if I did I would wind up on death row next to a redneck named Lawrence whose main goal was to give me a back rub before bed. I was frustrated and alone, and it was a familiar place. It is what I had felt in my public high school.

When I was sentenced for my arrest, on top of paying a ton of money and receiving three years of probation and losing my license for a bit, I was sent to a six-month outpatient treatment center, twice a week, twenty dollars a pop, piss test every Tuesday. I was told I have a disease. A sickness. And they were right. I do have dis-ease. We all do. It is a dis-ease of the mind, and it's called the ego. We are possessed by it. But the present day version of me says they were wrong about the powerless part. We are not powerless. None of us are. We are the exact opposite of that. We just have to believe it!

Growing up, I had good parents and a decent home life, but I think I always felt forced into the norm. That's what we do, isn't it? Most of us force our children to go to school because we are being forced to go to work and from this we grow resentful of one another. We bitch about our bosses or about taxes or about our hours or about our coworkers and we have to constantly fight to bring ourselves back to a peaceful state of mind, lest we shall perish in misery. We have no choice in that matter, or I suppose we do. There is always a choice, but once the little cherubs are involved then that choice becomes very limited. When there are mouths to feed at home, certain freedoms become nothing more than a picture on the wall or an ad in a travel magazine. This does not have to be the reality, though.

As I was alluding to before, to this day, I occasionally enjoy a steady toke of the God-given greenery. You know what I'm saying? That marijuana, that skunk, that herb, that sticky green plant that grows out of the ground that makes you happy and hungry and relaxed. The difference between now and then is that I understand the way my own mind works. Over the last six or seven years, I've learned some of my own inner wiring, studied my own personality traits, and most important, recognized my weaknesses, and I took the steps to change them. But how, you might ask? Well, it wasn't easy, but I made a commitment to myself and to my responsibility for my human counterparts.

I decided that I would no longer serve my mind, but rather my mind would serve me. I started sitting, meditating, exploring, researching, and most important, loving my soul and my life. I started believing in not believing, and I allowed the universe to invade my bloodstream and transform my semihappy, secretly depressed, and utterly imbalanced way of living. I recognized that my greatest enemy was, and still is, my own ego, and I started taking the steps to destroy it. I stopped living the way I was programmed to live, and I started to download brand new software to my motherboard. It is software that is available and pertinent at all times, rich in knowledge and above all else, 100 percent free. I started to live the way I was meant to and not the way I was told to. I started to become my intuition, and that's exactly what we need to teach our future generations!

Unfortunately for us, many times we put these crucial, life-transforming, self-empowering ideas on our children's back burners for the most influential segment of their lives. Instead of using formative years to help them *form* their own being, we use it to demand they form a perception of what we believe to be correct. And when they don't meet the criteria, we project our own adult weaknesses and fears onto them. These are fears that we formed when we were younger, most likely due to the same projections being cast onto us by the adults in our lives! It's cyclical—or *sick*lical—and we must break this pattern before it completely breaks us.

Where is the textbook that says, "Study thyself and learn *your* truth," or the worksheet that reads, "Self-love conquers all hatred and leads to a better us?" We need to make a drastic change in the way we approach our "educational" system, and by drastic, I mean we need to throw the whole fucking thing in the Dumpster, or at least three-quarters of it. This chapter was fun to write. Thanks for hanging in there.

It looks like a group of strippers had their holiday party in the kindergarten room. There's goddamn glitter everywhere. This is why I get asked questions when I get home late with glitter on my face, smelling of baby wipes and fucking GoGo SqueeZ.

14

Psyches, Psychos, and Sega Genesis

The problem with being bored without self-awareness is that it puts the mind in a state of craving. It makes us want something—anything other than what we have. It opens the door to impulsive choices and hasty decisions. I have this, but I want that. I needed this, but now that I've got it, I need that other thing. This isn't good enough; that must be better, so let me buy that because it will make me happy, temporarily...until I'm unhappy again. Just like that, we tumble down the rabbit hole of imaginary contentment and pleasure. We chase the addiction, the craving of mythical titillation, as if the answer to happiness is hiding just behind the next door, and the next one, and the next.

The psyche of a young person is complex and sporadic. It is like Sonic The Hedgehog all strung out on cocaine and meth, spiraling fast, rolling downhill, and flying off jumps. There are days when I look at my daughter, and I say to myself, "This girl's brain is like a fucking World War Two kamikaze pilot." Her mind just flies around at treacherous speeds until inevitably, it hits something and explodes. Sometimes the explosion is laughter, sometimes tears, and sometimes a straight-up, goddamn hissy fit. For the most part, kids want what they want NOW, and once they get it, they want something else. They grow bored easily because they don't have the ability to comprehend that this life is routine in many ways. Humor me for a moment...

There are certain things that we can refer to as *natural routines* and other things that are *cultural routines*. The sun comes up. The sun goes down. The body gets tired; it sleeps; it wakes; it eats; it moves; it takes a big old dookie; it gets tired. Repeat. From an observational standpoint, this would seem to be natural routine. Take a look at your dog or cat. I bet they've mastered the art of this specific routine.

Cultural routines can be seen as those activities that revolve around a clock. Drop the kids off, go to work, eat lunch, leave work, visit the therapist, get the kids, go to sports practice. Then there's dinner at six, TV show at seven, shower by eight, bed by nine. It's a conditioning of the mind that is passed down from generation to generation, and it's strange and curious. We have to teach our kids that just because boredom is a part of life, it doesn't necessarily have to be in control of our abilities to remain grounded and disciplined, and furthermore, life doesn't have to be boring!

I'm gonna go out on a limb here and say that children, for the most part, are bored out of their skulls while at school. They are unable to focus on the tasks at hand, and because of this they give up, act out, and tell teachers to blow it out their ass or up their ass, or whatever you are in to. I don't judge.

The same exact thing we do as adults when we say, "Ah, fuck this, who cares, I don't need to do this shit," is what we tell children they aren't allowed to do in a classroom. Instead, we teach them to accept being unhappy in this particular social setting with phrases like "too bad," "get over it," and "life's not fair," so when they get older, they know how to bring the same acceptance to working a job that they don't really enjoy and living a life believing "that's just the way it is." It's one of the most hypocritical elements of adulthood: the notion that children aren't allowed to behave in certain ways, but we are!

I am talking about behavior, not responsibility. They are two different things. Behavior is human, barbaric, raw, unfiltered, and incessant. It's that split second between anger and tranquility, that moment when we feel something change inside us, rumbling in our belly, creeping up to our lungs and heart, looking to burst out of our mouth, hands, and limbs like fucked-up Teenage Mutant Ninja Turtles. It is the switch that turns us over from an understanding, attentive person to a hardheaded, malicious demon in the blink of an eye. We all have it, naturally present, and we learn the ways in which we choose to display such behaviors. Some of us are fortunate to learn how to display kindness, aptitude, and willingness through our behavior, and others learn to be malicious demons.

Responsibility, on the other hand, particularly in regard to our social settings, is something we must learn. We must have proper models to instill in us the *feeling* of responsibility that makes us want to be a willing participant in our particular community, whether at home or out and about in the world. We need to inject that feeling into our curriculum and give kids a chance to see that being emotionally responsible for one's own mind is a fantastic way to become self-reliant, compassionate, and balanced. With that said, can I get an 'amen'? Hell yeah, you can, Tim! Amen!

The poop that was left in the toilet in the boys' room turned the water into the color of antifreeze. Either that kid ate a fucking highlighter or his parents need to take him to a doctor, stat.

15

It was decided today by a grand jury that a white police officer who shot and killed an unarmed black teenager in Ferguson, Missouri, several months ago will not be brought up on charges for the young man's death. I am consciously deciding not to place names to this story as the names of those involved are not important and will simply, in your mind, separate them from their humanness and make them become "someone else" to you, when in truth, they *are* you, as I am you and you are me. Context and subject are at the core of all matters.

While the media has done what it always does (manipulate, lie, add fuel to the fire of its own pathetic agenda, subconsciously mind-fuck the population into believing everything they hear on the television) the people on the streets have rallied, looking for answers and searching for a type of resolution, while law enforcement has done what it usually does in cases like this: stayed relatively silent and issued a statement that they are "looking into it." Any bit of truth to make sense of what seems to be another senseless and tragic death has been washed away by too many opinions, poisoned emotions, and painful thoughts. Most violent deaths are senseless in that the people involved can easily avoid the conflict that leads to tragedy if only they didn't lack the proper self-discipline to do so.

In this particular incident, who knows what truly happened? The unfortunate answer to that is: only two people. One of them has been dead for months, his body riddled with twelve bullet holes, sprawled on the pavement for hours on end before anyone even attended to him, blood spilling from his body like water from a dam. The other is left to live with what he has done. Self-defense or unjustified, his soul is left to rot among the living, most likely never to sleep an honest night's sleep again. He may be afraid to leave his own house to go the corner store for a cup of shitty coffee, but rest assured that he will collect his pension, paid for by the same taxpayers who rally against him, which is a shining example of life's cruel ironies.

Let us indulge in a hot bowl of reality soup! In America, we currently live under the broken umbrella of a system that thrives off hatred and racism. A system that is so awash with stories of the murders of human beings whose skin shades are not white that we are unable to reverse our notions of what equality actually means. Yes, we are all equal in the eyes of the universe or God, or whatever the fuck you want to call it, but *no*, we are certainly not equal in the eyes of many judges and lawyers, *some* police officers, corrections officers, and the corporate elitists who plot wars and steal our money. This seems to me an undeniable reality, and I welcome any argument proving otherwise.

An overwhelming majority of prisoners are black and Latino, many in jail for nonviolent drug offenses. These are the same kinds of offenses that most white Americans get away with or are given lenient sentences like probation or a fine or the proverbial slap on the wrist. It is good to note that white people use drugs at the same rate or more as black and Latino people, but the incarceration rates for people of color is staggering. Do you think it is by chance that prisons happen to be filled with poor people of color, or is it by design?

If this is indeed the land of the free, then why do we have the highest incarceration percentage on the planet? Am I making that up? Maybe I am, maybe I'm not. You can certainly research it for yourself and obtain enlightenment on the matter. By teaching our children that racism died with slavery, we are irresponsible. It coincides with the "idea of fact" that I touched on already. Consider it another example of the myths that are the backbone of our public school model: Columbus discovered America,

Lee Harvey Oswald shot JFK on his own, Abraham Lincoln opposed slavery, the Founding Fathers believed in equality for *all*, etc. If we continue to play the game of telephone in our schools by simply repeating what we've been told is true without gifting our children the tool of objectivity, then we have nowhere to go but off the cliff into the bottomless abyss of calamity and failure.

The biggest tragedy behind the Ferguson case mentioned above is that inside these public school walls (these green-tiled, hospital-like, glossy concrete walls), where cardboard cutouts and poster boards praising the elitist gods and devils for providing us our liberties, where children hang signs about how great their country is because it allows them freedom of choice—or rather, some choice—and where teachers recycle the same "lessons" every year; inside these walls, not one child is taught about the reality of life "out there." The notion of the real world goes no further than college, job, Disney World, having kids, vacation once in a while, retirement, travel if you're lucky, unretire if you're not, retire again, and then finally, hopefully, die peacefully. Why do we skip over realities so often? How come we don't talk about college tuition being a complete farce? How come we don't talk about Disney World being the biggest rip-off in the Western hemisphere? (Please note that it is inevitable that we will take the kids there for vacation, and I understand there might be some hypocrisy behind such action.)

In a classroom setting, we never mention how most of us as adults are completely disenchanted with the present political system, yet we continue to teach that our form of government is based on a two-party system, which it isn't, and that our vote really matters, which it doesn't. In the history of elections in America, the person with the most money has won every...single...time. Comedian Russell Brand suggested that we do away with the entire voting process, save ourselves some time, and just give the nod to whoever raises the most money because the one who has the most *always* wins. Seems logical to me.

Are we as adults simply convinced that we are being treated fairly, or do we settle for semihappiness in a partially fulfilling existence and, more important, are we really in a position to ensure freedom to our children's future? Is this, this thing we call *life*, and are *we* an illusion we have created through centuries of denial of our true selves? Are we all one? Are we—strange human atoms spinning on a rock that floats in space among billions upon billions of other rocks—are we simply this, or are we more than this?

What do we have to do to open up the dialogue between parents, teachers, students, and administrators in order to drop all the bullshit, all the made-up happiness and genuine fear, so that we can start to make real progress? Quite simply, when do we become REAL with one another? These are serious questions that call for honest answers. If you are a mother or father, then perhaps it is time to ask, "Who do I want my child to grow up to be?" And then it's time to be that person yourself.

"You say you want a revolution—well, you know...you better free your mind instead." Sir Paul McCartney, you fucking rock.

It perplexed the crap out of me. Meaning, I literally thought about it while taking a poop.

16

Random Negative Thoughts from My Inner Space

Thought Up while Cleaning the Outer Space

1. WE ARE DESTROYING OUR PLANET and simultaneously creating generation after generation of dumbed-down, desensitized, disconnected humans. The current model that is in place is an abysmal failure and will continue to be so as long as we choose our salary over our children's future. Who am I talking to? I have no clue, but a guilty conscience needs no accuser. I seriously don't want to sweep these steps right now. Ugh.

2. Don't worry, kids, you will be safe as long as you know your role, do exactly what you're told, and shut up while you're doing it. Don't think and don't speak. Just work, sleep, repeat, and hand over your hard-earned money so we can buy more bullets and bombs. Jesus, this room looks like a scene from that movie *Twister*.

3. Black, white, red, yellow, purple, blue. All these colors resemble labels. Labels formed by ignorant minds and false egos. False egos make us believe and belief makes us act like shitty assholes to one another. Shitty...smelly...butts.

There are two places that the rich, powerful elite never send their children. One is war, and the other is public school. Therefore, it only makes sense that the greatest percentage of young men and women who kill and get killed in war attended public school.

Cleaning up after adults makes me never want to be one.

17

Inferiority Complex, Superiority Nonsense

"Sir, yes, Sir! You are my superior, Sir! Even though you treat me like a dickhead, I will still obey your every command, Sir!"

Our fear-filled inferiority complex is something that deserves attention. Like a spiritual plague handed down over centuries of dick-swinging, warrior-posturing, and horseback-riding male chauvinism, the ego has taken hold in the belly of what once was sticks, stones, swords, and fistfights, now replaced by bullets, bombs, missiles, and drones. It's a strange relationship, the male propensity to violence—the desire to prove who is the hardest, meanest, and toughest dude in the room on any given night. I purposely speak of the male gender because when reflecting on kings, dictators, presidents, generals, chiefs, warriors and the like, we can't avoid the conclusion that throughout history the greatest majority of war and violence has been the direct result of males' decisions to rape, burn, and loot, all for the sake of material and personal gain. Dudes simply can't help themselves from acting like dominant, territorial-ass clowns, unless of course you are Hillary Clinton, in which case you would be a dudess but an ass clown nonetheless.

With the evolution of the human being, our societal roles have shifted, and many women nowadays also display a certain level of aggression, be it in fast cars, playing sports traditionally intended for men to play (whatever the heck that means) and overall confidence and belief in their ability to get shit done. All things work best when in balance and quite frankly, a lot of the dudes that have been, presently are, and will be in positions of power in the future are fucking idiots and lack the clarity to see past their innate belligerence. I think this rant calls for some class participation.

Please answer the following question in essay form. Be sure to include an introduction, body, and conclusion, and cite all your references. You will have as much time as you want to complete this assignment.

> If dominance and superiority is a natural tendency that all creatures are born with, then are we humans, the creators of a super unhealthy and toxic trait of ego-based mental supremacy (that has us convinced that one piece of dirt holds more value than another piece of dirt), afraid to change this trait, or are we simply unaware that it exists? Why or why not?

Animals in the wild are extremely territorial. This is obvious to anyone who watches the behavior of domesticated dogs. When my dog, the beautiful bitch that she is, sees another dog walking past our house, she goes into a frenzy. If there were no front door between her and that other dog, she would do her best Usain Bolt impression down the steps and across my front lawn, and then try her darnedest to beat that other pup into submission. Of course, not all dogs are like this, and seemingly different temperaments are assigned to different species and then further allocated to each individual creature of said species, but my dog happens to be a fucking psycho. But then again, all dogs are the same, but not, in the same way all humans are the same, but not. It is all the same, yet different, yet the same, and now we are back to that old yin-and-yang theme.

In my expert opinion—yes, I've decided to give myself the title of *expert* on this matter. Why? Why not? Live a little, people!—my dog is acting purely on instinct and unconscious electrical impulse. It's like that place that we as parents go to when we think our child is in danger. It's that place that can make a killer out of even the holiest of holies. Operating in the red, no thought, all reaction, blacked out on anger and fear and protective intuition—a universal trait, rooted in fear, shared by all creatures. The difference between us and a dog seems to be that we have evolved to possess a deeper mental capacity in terms of harnessing good or bad emotions, self-control, decision-making abilities, etc., although one quick glimpse at the world might change your mind about that. This is not a newly discovered notion that I have stumbled on while cleaning pencil markings off desks. Psychologists, psychiatrists, philosophers, and scientists have been figuring out the complexities of the human mind for centuries.

It has also been found that primates and other species have a capacity for more critical thinking and reactivity, and therefore they can display "human emotion" such as compassion, sadness, joy, anger, and so on. The term *human emotion* certainly says a lot about how bloody highly we think of ourselves. We have even laid claim to an invisible idea called emotion, like it is ours and the rest of the life that inhabits the earth simply borrows what we own. But we don't own it; we just act like the neighborhood bully and say we do. We've created a falsehood about who we are and how important we are, and we believe it! By God, we believe it with all our might! It's like this…

We humans happen to be the ones with the most weapons, so at this point in the earth's history, we are the ones who are deciding who lives where, what creatures will live, what species will perish, and what resources we will deplete. It's pretty heavy when you think of it in those terms. When you stop what you are doing (stop your life and your mind) and take a few minutes to observe, you will quickly realize that we are fucking up royally, and if we don't figure out a way to fix it, then eventually, somewhere down the road, our great-great-great-grandchildren are going to suffer, or prosper, depending on our decisions we make *now*.

What I am conveying, again in the form of a question, and for the sake of sparking something to ruminate on, is this:

Why do we feel the need to consider ourselves more important than the next creature? Why are we conditioned to give titles, form a hierarchy, and follow a select few? Is it a natural law that one must rule and the rest must obey, or is there something based on fear that is culturally dictated to us that makes us say yes when we are certain we should say no?

Why do I think the idea of having a title that suggests someone is superior to others, at work, in school, in the army, at the car wash, or in Chucky Cheese (by the way, fuck that place and all its expensive video games and sweatshop-made prizes) is unhealthy and counterproductive? Why do I, a *man* who wipes the shit off tile floors and who acts like Mr. Belvedere for a living, why do I think claiming a position of power is utter nonsense? Simple. It's nonsense because we are truly, undeniably, all equal, but a huge percentage of us have no knowledge of this.

This lack of depth and perceptual awareness leads to an inferiority complex so deeply rooted in the world's history that most of us find more comfort living a frightened existence, caught up in an emotional game of hide and seek. We hide how and who we really are, and we seek the answers to how and who we think we should be from someone perceived to be greater than us, stronger than us, and smarter than us. It's a lie. It always has been, since before Genghis Khan convinced his men to burn children and women and before America dropped an atomic bomb on thousands of the same.

We are, for the most part, composed of the same matter. All of us are made up of blood and guts, head and heart, bone and flesh, energy and force. Inside us and inside our children is something animalistic and beautiful, deep at the core, hibernating, ready to manifest the change the world needs. A revolution does not happen overnight. It happens over lifetimes. We need to show our young ones, teach them how to harness their capacity to overcome this archaic system, this seeping facade, to create a new life force together as a tribe, a family, and a human organism.

When I was a younger man, as in when I was in my twenties and not my thirties, I worked for a very well-known parcel delivery service. It was a union job with full benefits and a 401k, equipped with all the hoopla that ropes us in to working for the same company doing the same thing every day for twenty, twenty-five, thirty years, half-miserable, half-suicidal, half-alive. It was a grueling and physical job. I would load trucks overnight in order for them to be ready for delivery by 8:00 a.m. Part of the job requirement was to be able to load an average of two hundred packages or more an hour. I would average anywhere from eight hundred to twelve hundred boxes a shift.

After about three years in this particular setting, I experienced back problems, shoulder problems, and general pain from the wear and tear of the job. I have always stayed in shape (with the exception of when I was nineteen and was pretty much wasted every day for about a year) always trained hard, whether in the gym, on a field, or on a mat. Being active is something I enjoy, but this particular place kicked my ass something awful. I had to learn over time how to stop trying to meet the ridiculous demands of a company whose only concern is their bottom line and their stock value, and I had to stop being afraid of the consequences of not meeting my daily quota. I took some huge steps in personal growth because I realized that a fear of anything—and in this particular case, fear of the company higher-ups—leads to real unhappiness. It makes us do things for all the wrong reasons.

What exactly was I afraid of? Not moving packages fast enough? Not placing the boxes in a sufficiently symmetrical pattern on the shelves? Was I afraid that I was going to lose my job or be labeled as lazy, or was I afraid of being "written up" on a paper report of my poor work ethic that would be cast into a never-ending file cabinet filled with write-ups of other people's shitty work ethics? I mean, really? What are we all afraid of? It's an important question to think about and one that will lead many of us to the same answer: death.

We are afraid to die, and that ingrained fear that is embedded so far in our psyches that we are unable to make amends with it as the *only real truth* makes us live a life of mental slavery. I was essentially afraid of nothing; I was terrified of human models and systems and bullshit. I was afraid because I was taught to be afraid. Yes. That's it. I was living in fear of made up human bullshit...and death.

In my six and a half years of employment there I had a slew of supervisors, managers, bosses, etc. whom I had to answer to, listen to, oblige, and appease. It didn't matter if their commands and demands were farcical, impossible, or downright incompetent. When the boss said jump, most of us said, "How high?"

It's the same mentality that plagues the world. Someone in a position of power tells a group of people to do something, and no matter how god-awful or asinine the request may be, the people oblige because they fear the punishment more than they care about the result. It's a pathological sickness that takes root in these schools, and it is so deep-rooted that the only way to start fresh is to cut every one of these red-brick, mosaic-floored trees down and plant new seeds. We need to plant seeds that aren't injected with an authoritative agenda and an indoctrinated life force. That's the only way.

A child wrote on the bathroom wall, "I'm going to have a bomb party." The word bomb, in this instance, is used descriptively, meaning good or amazing or huge. Naturally, one of the higher-ups in the administration called the police because they thought this meant that a student was literally going to have a party with bombs in the school.

18

Quiet, Quiet, Quiet Halls, Children Bouncing off the Walls; Back and Forth They Walk All Day, Afraid to Speak, Afraid to Play

One good thing about music, when it hits, you feel no pain.

—ROBERT MARLEY

It's quiet around these parts. Sometimes it's too quiet. Quiet like penitentiary halls during lights out. Quiet like church when everyone is kneeling, then sitting, then standing, then kneeling again. What the fuck is that all about, anyway? Sit, stand, kneel, sit, stand, kneel, give us your money, sit, stand, kneel again! Okay. Bye! Be sure to leave some money on the way out. See ya next week! Remember, Jesus loves you, but only if you come back next week to give us more money!

There should be music playing over the PA every day, blasting through the hallways, blaring from the loudspeaker. There should be weekly concerts in the gym so kids can dance and celebrate, real tribal-like, with drums and sticks and shakers and weird voodoo masks all laced up on LSD in search of the fourth or fifth dimension, swinging from the curtains on the stage, climbing through the rafters. Yes, that's when the real education will commence. Kids should be able to sing aloud, off-key and offbeat, and beat their tiny chests like our ancestors did. They should have background music to every scene portrayed in this bizarre institution. They should be studying the lyrics of Marley and Burning Spear and infusing their cells with the rhythms of Femi Kuti. Yes!

What they need is a soundtrack, but not a shitty, watered-down pop-radio soundtrack (unless it's Bruno Mars), but a soundtrack filled with vibrant beats and killer grooves. It should have style like Miles Davis and get down like James Brown. It should funk like George Clinton and invoke like George Harrison. Or maybe it should be hard and gritty, like Wu Tang Clan's "36 Chambers" or Public Enemy's "Fuck the Police." Students should be able to express without feeling oppressed, release without feeling defeat. Fuck, yeah. Or how about we start playing the music you hear in yoga class—Krishna Das and Sounds of Nature—so the waterfalls and ocean waves crashing over the speakers will remind everyone that there is an entire planet out there that needs saving. Teachers and students can get all *namaste* and flexible and start doing downward dog or eagle pose in the middle of their state-issued "fear exams." Yep, fear exams. Not sure what it means, but I like it, and I just felt like Clint Eastwood in my head when I said it, so it sticks. Badass motherfucker. Let's not forget about the really heavy stuff. Hardcore, screamo music that makes teenagers clash and collide in mosh pits until all their angst is drained from their lost souls, melted away in a puddle of prepubescent dirt and sweat. Maybe we can have a mosh pit in the principal's office. He's pretty cool and might even take a selfie while we are at it. Hell, yes. Welcome to my school. Your education begins *now*.

Good god. This bathroom smells like a cross between the Superdome post-Katrina and that portable bathroom that I sniffed blow in at that concert on Randall's Island thirteen years ago. What the fuck do these kids eat for lunch? Oh, that's right—pizza and milk.

THE ESSENTIAL CUSTODIAL PLAYLIST

1. Bob Marley—"Wake Up and Live"
2. Brother Ali—"Daylight"
3. Chaka Khan—"Never Miss the Water"
4. 311—"Unity"
5. Miles Davis—"Jeru"
6. Merle Haggard—"I Can't Stop Loving You"
7. Incubus—"Deep Inside"
8. Band of Horses—"Is There a Ghost"
9. Hector Lavoe—"El Cantante"
10. Rage Against the Machine—"Testify"
11. Masters at Work—"You Can Do It, Baby"
12. Zero 7—"In the Waiting Line"
13. Burning Spear—"Marcus Garvey"
14. The Doors—"Moonlight Drive"
15. Ray LaMontagne—"Shelter"
16. Pink Floyd—"Time"
17. Blind Melon—"Mouth Full of Cavities"
18. Citizen Cope—"Son's Gonna Rise"
19. The Beatles—"While My Guitar Gently Weeps"
20. Elton John—"I Guess That's Why They Call It the Blues"
21. Damian Marley—"Road to Zion"
22. Johnny Cash—"Ring of Fire"
23. TOOL—"Wings for Marie"
24. The New York Dirt—"Man without a State"
25. Bruno Mars—"Liquor Store Blues"
26. Amy Winehouse—"Stronger Than Me"
27. Red Hot Chili Peppers—"Knock Me Down"
28. Stevie Wonder—"As"
29. Jimmy Cliff—"Rivers of Babylon"
30. Peter Tosh—"I Am That I Am"
31. Atmosphere—"God Loves Ugly"

32. Birds of Tokyo—"Lanterns"
33. The Black Crowes—"Seeing Things"
34. Robert Bruey—"Dorian"
35. Champion The City—"Come Down"
36. Moon Tooth—"Storm Pill"
37. Flobots—"Mayday"
38. Foo Fighters—"Dear Rosemary"
39. Goapele—"Closer"
40. Karnivool—"Roquefort"
41. Manu Chao—"Clandestino"
42. J. Cole—"Hello"
43. Exemption—"Bleeding Blue"
44. Phil Collins—"Invisible Touch"
45. 311—"Omaha Stylee"
46. The Police—"The Bed's Too Big Without You"
47. Black Coffee, featuring Bucie—"Superman"
48. Hall & Oates—"Can't Go For That"
49. Black Dub—"I Believe in You"
50. 311—"1, 2, 3"

19

Lice, Lice, Baby

Critters, Jitters, Man Buns, and the New Age Bully Movement

I live in a household made up of five humans, one dog, three fish, two life-size Anna and Elsa dolls from the movie *Frozen*, which I have seen so many times—I'm sure like many of you—it makes me want to simultaneously throw up and beat the shit out of every single Disney employee currently working at, on, or in the Magic *Fucking* Kingdom, three bedrooms, four too many bathrooms, an office that my significant other aptly named the "muddy" because it doubles as a mudroom, which really means "a place for the kids to throw all their shit on the floor," and a study, in which I sit and pretend I am doing something scholarly and smart while I watch break dancing and mixed martial arts videos. It also includes a front room, back room, dining room, kitchen, basement, front porch, backyard, front yard, garage, swing set, and anything else this peculiar and oft-shallow suburbanite setting calls for! Do me a favor and reread that entire section in one breath to get the full effect of my fitful emotion. Done? Good job.

My girlfriend/fiancée and I have been together for a good while. Before we were together, she was married and made babies, and I didn't. Over the years, those babies have turned into an eleven-year-old boy and eight-year-old identical-twin girls. It's good to note that she didn't make babies by herself like that woman who was a virgin and birthed a child.

No, I'm not talking about Mary the mama of Jesus. I'm talking about Isis, the mama of Horus, who by many accounts was also a virgin when she dropped old Horus onto the earth. Didn't hear about that one yet? Well, supposedly that took place long before the whole Jesus thing started. History, history, who are you now?

Anyway, you'll be happy to know that my wife has a "baby daddy" who is still active and present in the lives of his children, and the entire situation is quite remarkable. I'm not all insecure and weird about it. It is a part of life, and sometimes life happens, so you have to man up, believe in your path, and play the part. Do what you can, while you can, until you can't anymore. Then move on. Simple. We all get along swimmingly as that is the only way it should be when kids are involved. If you are a parent who has gone through a divorce, and you aren't mature enough to put your own personal shit to the side for the sake of the kids, then you should seriously reconsider what you are doing, stop being an immature asshole, and move on.

So while the three beautiful cherubs that I have the pleasure to share most of my life with are not "technically" mine, they are, spiritually and universally, certainly part of me. They are assuredly mine in many ways. Not mine as in I own them, but mine as in I keep them as part of me, many days selfishly protective, circling like a hawk, trying to guard them from the hideousness of this fucked-up society, trying to show them the brilliance of this amazing world, trying to infuse them with morals and ideals that center around balance and love and emotional health. They are every bit a part of me as the spirits see fit, and taking on the role of a parent, guardian, stepfather, father, and being the only adult with dreadlocks and tattooed knuckles at the lacrosse field has been almost inexplicable and a never-ending self-learning process. I'm not sure that words suffice to voice what I feel to be responsible in some ways for three human lives. It's fucking bizarro sometimes, and intriguing, and fast.

As people, we take on roles. We assign labels to everything. We fall in love with our story, rituals, routines, and our idea of self. We commit to our ideas with unwavering certainty. We don't want to hear criticism. We abandon objectivity for emotional impulse. As parents, we add more fuel to this fire, more connection to others, more commitment to our belief system, and more desire to make sure everything is always perfect. And for many of us, we strive day in and day out to provide something healthier for our kids, something based on freedom that contains the true power of expression and exploration, and we do this even when they are being a pain in the dick or vagina—or both, if you are so endowed.

Interpersonal relationships have the tendency to be like rough seas. The head is the boat, and the thoughts inside it are the passengers being thrown about, slamming into the walls, panicking, gasping for air, doing anything to find their way to a safer and more stable place. I expect that it's hard enough for a lot of us in the adult world to maintain healthy relationships with other adults daily. When we work the same job and see the same people all the time for hours and days on end, sometimes signals start to cross and interweave. From this a foundation is placed, made up of a bag of psychological concrete. Once it is put in place we build on to it year after year, until we are satisfied with what we have established. Only for most of us, we are not satisfied for long. We want to change this or fix that, or add this or take out that. We want it, them, the world, to be different, better, more relaxing, easier to get along with. But it can't be so, because we believe that happiness will come in the form of "things," and not just physical things, but emotional, mental, and spiritual things as well, and it won't. Happiness is not fleeting, but happiness all the time is. There must be hardships in order to know exactly what real happiness is. Overcoming struggle is an essential ingredient in developing a character made of compassion and strength. It is inside this life lesson that head lice and the man bun presented their expertise.

It was a cold, dark Sunday with rain battering the windows and lightning striking down young children as they ran for the car in the Toys"R"Us parking lot. There were structure fires, gale-force winds, and hail the size of baseballs—no, softballs—no, fucking bowling balls! Godzilla and King Kong collided in front of Panera Bread (only after they shared that soup thing in a bread bowl, which is freaking fantastic), and a *Tyrannosaurus rex* came crashing through with Elvis and Tupac Shakur on its back, both scratching their heads to find relief from the horrific infestation known as *Pediculus humanus capitis*: lice.

It is every parent's worst nightmare, creepy crawlers setting up camp on the scalp of their most precious gifts, causing discomfort, paranoia, and an automatic itchiness that spreads like an oil spill! Isn't it curious how the minute a child in your presence is discovered with lice your own scalp starts tightening, you start freaking out, and you begin scratching imaginary itches like a crackhead withdrawing from the rock? Immediately, all articles of clothing and household linens are placed in black garbage bags and firebombed in the backyard. Simultaneously all hoods go on, the hair goes up, and the hazmat suits are donned, giving the impression that the filming of *Back to the Future 4* is about to begin in the kitchen. This all takes place only after driving 100 miles per hour to the pharmacy to get the head-lice–cocktail kit, complete with a number for a trauma hotline for those of us parents who don't do well in these types of situations. This was the scene, only maybe less exaggerated, in my household not too long ago, and this is how it played out.

THE PONYTAIL KID
The boy is ten years old, and he has long blond hair. His hair is beautiful, like a lion on the cover of an African safari brochure, making love to a cheetah. Actually, picture the *Lion King* version of *Caligula*. That makes no sense at all, but I'm leaving it! Anyhow, I call him "Neckbone" or "Neck" for short. I'll admit I stole that nickname from a movie called *Mud* starring Matthew McConaughey—who, by the way is a fucking stud of an actor—but it just fit so perfectly that I decided to use it. In retrospect, I use it so much that I don't even remember what his real name is. I think his name is something with a vowel in it and two or three syllables. His mom knows for sure.

Neck was the first one of the three kiddies to say those four ghastly, hair-raising words: "My head is itchy." Fuck, shit, goddamn it, NO! "Stand here, don't move!" Armed with a flashlight and a comb we began the search. Hair by hair, follicle by follicle, we examined his treasured scalp, and sure enough we started to find little tiny bugs, crawling around, acting like annoying dickheads.

Naturally, the first words out of his mouth were, "Am I going to have to cut my hair?" He was terrified at the thought of this. Not so much because he likes having long hair, but more because he was afraid of what other kids would think. He was petrified at the idea of having to face his classmates and explaining that the reason he had to chop his hair off was because he had lice. He was afraid of being ridiculed for something he couldn't control, of trying to explain that he is still cool, even though his physical appearance had changed overnight. It was sad to hear and an eye-opener for me.

Why are we forcing our children into social situations that they might not be ready for? Why aren't we providing them tools of confidence and self-assurance instead of being lackadaisical in our attitude toward the system? I know that it's easy for adults to say that cruelty among humanity is just part of the world and that children have to figure it out for themselves and "just deal with it," but what if this train of thought is wrong? What if we figured out a way to first deal with our own fears and insecurities as parents, adults, role models, teachers, leaders, whatever, and became true examples of what and how a compassionate and civilized community should be? Is this even possible, or are we too far gone? Yes, there is a natural darkness to the world, prevalent throughout history in people like Josef Stalin and Dick(head) Cheney, but there is also a much brighter and stronger side. I believe that people genuinely want to be nice for the most part. Most humans want to live in peace; they are just taught that there *has* to be war and violence and stress and strife. I'm not so sure.

I think this is a notion based on centuries of inherited fear. All children start with a blank slate, an opportunity to grow into a kind and loving individual, and it is really a matter of how much shit the adults in their lives decide to dump into that child's psyche, how much conscious thought the elder brings to the table when raising a kid, that determines the outcome. There is a saying that goes, "The world only has ten bad people in it.

They just keep moving around." Maybe they just keep moving through our public schools. Moving on.

We took the kids to a place called the Fairy Lice Mothers. I know, what a brilliant business name, right? Talk about cornering a market and making a killing; kudos to the founder of a business that would make most people hightail it the other way. Cleansing the heads of strangers all day to rid them of lice is not something most people aspire to, but at two hundred bucks a head, fuck yeah, make that money and get your bling on. And although it was expensive, it was extremely informative and well beyond the worth. Not only were they able to get rid of all the nastiness and give us a follow-up plan to ensure we exterminated all the lice, they also passed along some really useful knowledge about how to treat the problem without become obsessive freaks. Did you know lice do not jump? They climb. And all those rumors about having to bag your entire wardrobe up? Nonsense.

One of the most important guidelines that we had to follow was making sure the kids kept their hair up and in a ponytail for a week. The girls were fine with that, as they usually want some type of princess getup anyway, but the boy—well, the boy was panicked. We told him that putting his hair back actually allowed people to see his face. I told him that samurais and rock stars all wore ponytails and man-buns, and I even showed him pictures of Steven Segal in the nineties (just kidding, but has anyone found Bobby Lupo yet?) Needless to say, it helped to comfort him not one bit. He was so afraid of being made fun of that he actually begged us to keep him home. He also pouted, sulked, and put on an Oscar-worthy performance depicting how his classmates would make fun of him. It was a little dramatic but the essence of it was that he was genuinely freaking out.

It's hard to teach young minds about happiness, about embracing what is good and discarding what is not. Hell, it's hard to teach anybody that. Kids just want to be liked and popular and accepted. And they also want to fit in, for the most part. Again, they are *just like adults* in this matter. They want to be loved by all, and the thought of being made fun of causes anxiety, insecurities, and fear. And it is almost a guarantee that public school will, at some point or another, give every child these feelings.

But kids have always made fun of other kids, right? Isn't that all a part of growing up? Dealing with neighborhood bullies, learning to defend yourself, or choosing to walk away? Deciding if you want to be the better person? It's something that old, beaten-down war vets proclaim will make kids tough and build character. It shows them what the world is really about! I mean, yeah, maybe, but can't the world be something different from what it has always been? Isn't it up to us to decide that together?

The Neck went to school the next day like any other. Lacrosse shorts, hoodie, funky-ass socks pulled up to his ankles, kicks, schoolbag, and a ponytail. The next morning, as usual, I rolled up to the school drop-off spot at nine o'clock on the dot, leaning back in the front seat of my Volvo XC, and told the kids to jump out while I was still moving because I was in a rush, and it gives the school aides standing outside something to talk about. There is nothing more exhilarating than seeing a couple of kids come barreling out of the back door of a moving vehicle at nine in the morning. It's fucking hilarious every time. What? No one got hurt!

I went about my business for the day: manicure, pedicure, yoga class, cross fit, tai chi, tai kwon do, ate some Thai food, rock climbing, horse-back riding, table-tennis tournament at the YMCA, thespian meeting at the town theater, breakfast with the local news station, breakdance battle at the church, dog park, pet store, strip club to fill the vending machines with Mike and Ikes (my side hustle), Brazilian jiujitsu, Brazilian bikini wax, fed the pigeons, picked some pumpkins, watched *Funny Farm*—one of Chevy Chase's most underrated films, had a calendar photo shoot for the local 7-Eleven, and smoked a joint with the mailman. You know, pretty much the usual. Needless to say, by ten o'clock, I was freakin' exhausted.

It didn't take long before the nurse called. I had a feeling it was going to happen, but I wasn't exactly sure of what the reasoning behind the call would be. I thought maybe Neck would fake an illness and try to get out of there, which is a sad thought in itself, that a kid has to pretend to be sick because he is so unhappy being where he is (please note the correlation between that and what adults do at our own jobs as well), and knowing that he was having a tough time made part of me want to karate kick something or someone for the pettiness with which the world operates. It's very hard to describe what it feels like to know someone you love is in a place of emotional pain when all you can really do is observe from the outside and hope for the best. I'm sure you understand what I mean.

On the phone the nurse said she found him in the copy room, crying. It turns out that after I dropped the kids off, Neck, in an attempt to cover up his shame, put his hood up so as to hide his ponytail from the view of his classmates. It would seem that his plan backfired and the result was that everyone started asking him why he had his hood up and then maybe started teasing him about that. I cannot be 100 percent sure what happened as I was not there, but from what the nurse explained, a few classmates poked fun at him for whatever reasons, which resulted in him getting upset and his teacher having to have a talk with the class.

This all seems like pretty standard "kid stuff" to me, or even "human stuff." But in 2015, when the antibullying campaign is in full swing, can we, in fact, consider this bullying? Or is it simply kids being kids? Where did this antibullying thing come from? Do you know? Have you ever thought about it?

I've watched the antibullying movement grow over the years, and it seems to me that, as with most well-intended, popular campaigns, it is slowly turning into another method with which the thought police do their dirty work. In the wake of the Columbine High School shooting in April 1999, Georgia was the first state to pass antibullying legislation. What this means is that this was the first time that "bullying" was associated with *criminality*. This was, and still is, a very, slippery slope.

Go ahead. Say it. Why, Tim? Why is this a slippery slope? Why shouldn't we be able to take all these mean bullies and lock them away or expel them or suspend them? Why shouldn't we take a stand and let these prepubescent tyrants know that we will not tolerate such behavior? Why?

Well, for a few reasons. First and foremost, if we are talking about bullying in schools, then we are talking about dealing with children, not criminals. There is a fine line between impulsive, childlike decision making and committing a crime. Second, when we allow authoritative figures to start to dictate what language should be deemed offensive and bully-like, then it leads to a whole ton of politically correct bullshit that strips away freedoms and quite honestly turns our kids into a bunch of pussies who live in fear of anyone in an authoritative position. The message becomes "you can say this, but you can't say that," or "this is okay, but this isn't."

You ever wonder who makes up the rules? When I was a kid, I am pretty sure I was allowed to pack my Mattel cap gun in my backpack and bring it to school. In this day and age, if children so much as utter the word *gun* in school, there is a good chance they will find themselves being suspended, psychoanalyzed, and in some cases even arrested and charged criminally. We have let our paranoia completely overshadow our responsibility to our children and have failed them when it comes to creating a classroom and educational experience that they can trust.

We know that the world has a tendency to be cruel and that humanity has always had its share of bullies. One quick glance at today's global environment will show you that every world leader who sends young men and women to war is really just a bully hiding behind hired armies. At least a few centuries ago, kings and rulers would go out on the battlefield and fight alongside their battalions. Nowadays, these schmucks play war games from behind a computer screen and act like they are leading. It's the same all over. Grown men and women acting like insecure little dickheads, trying to prove who has more power. And that's exactly what a bully does! The bullies are telling us not to bully! It's bullyshit, for real.

So how do we counter this? I'm not exactly sure, but for my children, I start with instilling confidence and self-love every...single...day. I tell them they are stronger than they know, that they are loved and that more important, they have incredible abilities to love others as well. I also constantly knock them off their own pedestals by reminding them that they are human just like everyone else and that there is no end to the amount of work that must be done in order to improve as a person. I also remind them that they are not special. I tell them that someone who is trying to cause pain to another human being is, in all actuality, someone who is in pain and in need of the deepest love possible and that they need to learn how to navigate through their own painful waters as well. And I also tell them to figure out what their boundaries are and to decide for themselves how much they are willing to take. I tell them that violence is *never* an answer, even though sometimes I want to tell them that a bully needs to get punched right in his or her grille, and I tell them that this is all temporary and that the world needs *real* leaders who desire peace and unity via peace and unity, not armies and bullets. I think this is good parenting. I hope.

In the end, the Neckbone grew from his tangle with lice. He made it through and learned to love his ponytail. His skin grew thicker, but his heart became warmer. He even wears his hair up now from time to time. I, on the other hand, well, I am still freaking out every time we feel an itch.

THE NECK INTERVIEW

Q: Describe school in three words:

A: Silly, annoying, boring. I can learn most of that stuff in two hours without being there for six hours.

Q: Do you need a teacher?

A: Yes, I do need a teacher. But you or Mommy can teach me.

Diagnosis: This kid is brilliant.

20

Who Am I, and Why Do I Teach, and What Do I Teach, and How Do I Teach?

What does it mean to be a teacher? What qualities and ideals should a proper educator hold? What is education? Is it something that can only be found in classrooms and overpriced university libraries? Is it legitimized by a piece of paper hanging on the wall? Is education only found in the four basic subjects that every public school treads on, harps on, and harpoons its students with, leaving them bleeding from the ribs after twelve years of routine, forced behavior? If education is something found inside an institution bound together by tile, concrete, and asbestos-laden pipes, something invisible and only defined by human language, then when does it end? Does it cease to exist after grade school, after college, after death? Is it over once students step out of these red-brick buildings and into the "real world," as if their present world is a different world from the one we live in, like a wonderful fairy tale filled with gumdrop rainbows and the fucking Lollipop Kids singing their song, and not the real world that adults are used to (grown children with whiny voices found daily, grumbling and complaining next to the Keurig machine, drinking coffee and bitching about how much their job sucks and how the kids they teach are idiots and not worthy of their precious time)? (End rant)

What have *we* learned throughout our life that makes us so goddamn educated, anyway? Every kid I know can find happiness in something as simple as a sprinkler and as basic as a stick, so maybe they are the enlightened ones. And when is the last time you did long division, anyway?

The late great comedian George Carlin said, "Don't just teach your children to read, teach them to question what they read. Teach them to question everything." So, my friends, are we heeding this advice? Are we questioning everything? Are we expanding the conscious mind or retreating further from the truth into the bloody mess of politics and bureaucracy? What waters are we swimming in and why do we place our hopes in forms of government, be it this one or that one, thinking that the machine will throw us a life vest? How can we "be the change," really?

A good friend of mine asked me what a typical day would be like inside my classroom. It is a question that eludes me often as I firmly believe that before we can make any type of real progress, we must first abandon that which holds us back, keeps us trapped, and feeds the present systemic design. Things have been so flawed and so corrupted for so long that we have grown accustomed to living with instability, blinded by fear, moving in place. It is going to take a mass awakening, a revival filled with love and hope and all that hippie shit, to set us on a new course. (Maybe even a ton of hallucinogens and weed. Who's buying?)

I truly don't see a promising future for public schools unless we scale back, begin to explore the idea of privatizing, and tell the government to mind its own p's and q's. We can start small. The movement against standardized testing among parents and teachers is, in my opinion, an excellent sign of progress. Good teachers want to teach freely, and good students want to learn the same way. Eventually people get tired of being told what to do with the threat of being punished if they fail to comply, and that punishment almost always comes in the form of money. Governments are very good at blackmailing and coercing us into doing what they want us to do.

Of course, shitty teachers abound, and there are also awful human beings roaming the earth, but there is also an opposite for everything and I really believe that we, those pure of heart and sound of mind, can and will make a difference for our children. Let the mind of a child roam free for a day, and the earth shall become its playground. Boom!

At 7:20 a.m., hang the American flag up with Paulo, a seventy-two-year-old Italian man who immigrated to America over thirty years ago to pursue the American dream. Yes, he is seventy-two and still works full-time and never learned how to read or write English, but he seems to have done just fine for himself. So much for that early retirement plan.

21

Silent Marble

Skateboards, Drums, Ghosts, and Falling Posters

Some nights, when it gets late and all my work is done, I pretend that I'm at the quietest after-hours club on the planet, only I don't trip out on Ecstasy like I used to, although maybe I should to spice things up a bit. I play deep, soulful house music on my phone, grab my board, and I skate from one side of the building to the next. I keep all the lights off in the hallways, save for a few so I don't bust my ass or run into a concrete wall, and I enjoy my time alone. I just kick, push, and coast, like the rap artist Lupe Fiasco. It's a meditative process; one that brings me backward and forward to different places and times. It gets me out of "here" for a little while even though I am still here, bowing down to the time clock, collecting my check. This skateboard is the greatest antianxiety pill that I have ever seen.

Other nights I go wandering, looking for ghosts. Searching like a little kid, allowing myself to pretend I hear something, hoping that I will see something eerie or strange. I secretly wish for something to catch my eye. I don't necessarily believe in ghosts, but I believe in trying. It's desolate around here. Where am I? Who am I? What...are...we?

The basement underneath this building is expansive and unearthly. It's dirty, dark, and creepy, with huge furnaces, old furniture, computer equipment that looks like it was on that TV show *Lost*, lockers from the seventies, huge crawl spaces made up of dirt and concrete, old toilets and broken doors. Anytime I'm down there I think to myself, "I have to film a movie down here." It feels like Stephen King wrote the description for this place, and over the years the occupants of this building stuck to his script. It's splendid.

I don't ever expect to see ghosts, as in spirits floating around the building wearing sheets, which, by the way, always reminds me of the movie *Beetlejuice*, (all hail Geena Davis!), and I have never come in contact with any sort of apparition, but my friend George who used to work the night shift with me swears he has heard people talking in the distance late at night when he was in the building by himself. I guess I am looking more for an energy shift, a flicker of the light, or a door that suddenly swings open so I can tell my kids about the time at work I witnessed the undead. Or maybe I want to see it so I can say that working here was all worth it in the end, because I got to see the spirit of Carl, the janitor who died here in 1965 while cleaning the glass on the door of room 103. Yeah, that's the golden plunger—I mean ticket! Carl the janitor, the man, the myth, the legend, killed in the line of duty from inhaling too much ammonia. Poor Carl. You are my idol, man! Actually, none of that is fact, but Carl the ghost is as real as can be in my mind. I think I just saw his raggedy old ass. See, to be able to make it an adventure, no matter your surroundings—that's the key.

Things also fall apart around here seemingly on their own. Maybe it's the deceased who make the posters fall off the walls. When the building is in absolute silence, you can sometimes hear the projects made of poster board and construction paper that teachers hang on the walls hit the floor with a quiet thud. One by one, falling like leaves weighed down from an excessive use of glue and glitter.

Still other nights I wander into the greatest room to be found inside this bleary-eyed, concrete-walled fortress: the music room. Is there anything more powerful in this world than music? That sound, that vibration, that power of healing all delivered in one strum or strike, note or chord. It is the life force behind us all.

There is a drum set in the music room that was donated by a parent of one of our students. That parent also happens to be a custodian, once again proving that there is no limit to our desire to give back. It is a basic setup, consisting of a kick drum, snare drum, high hats, rack toms and a floor tom. If you have no idea what I'm talking about just picture Ringo Starr or another famous drummer on a drum set, then replace that image of Ringo with an image of your school custodian, then have a laugh at it.

I always start off grooving. *Boom clap, Ba boom-boom clap!* I feel the stick hit the drum, and I smile. I don't have to worry about anyone hearing my subpar drum playing because I am alone in this building, quarantined from the outside world. I am John Bonham with a set of keys hanging from my belt loop. I'm Neil Peart with a garbage can and Windex, and I'm in love. I'm in love with this room and its old drum set. I'm in love with its sound bouncing off the dropped ceiling, shaking the walls, making my ears ring. I'm in love with the way the thump from the bass drum simulates my pulse, and most of all, I am happy that the place I reluctantly spend much of my time in allows me the opportunity to at least create this rhythm. It is not a coincidence that I am responsible for the upkeep of the most important classroom in this building. For what the universe connects, music shall hold together.

The clock ticks, the heat bangs, and the mind wanders. It's just too bad these ghosts don't pick up all the shit they knock down.

Dear Play-Doh,
Even though I ingested you as a child, I fucking despise your messy ass now. Fuck you and the plastic container you rode in on.

22

It's Raining Cocks, Hallelujah!
It's Raining Cocks, Amen!

Gymnaphobia, Forest Escapades, and My Pal Dr. Bronner

To the group of kids who made the eight-foot-long snow sculpture of a penis and balls in the middle of the school yard, may I be the first to publicly say, "Bravo! I applaud your creativity and overall life ambition." Even though most people act like children at the mere mention of the word penis, or vagina for that matter, I find your work to be well thought-out and perfectly executed.

It is completely hilarious to me that nudity has evolved into something that is looked down on. Isn't it rather sad that we have become so insecure and hateful toward ourselves that many of us are afraid to accept our most natural form of physical self? Then again, this is coming from a guy who once took a shower on the back of a fire truck equipped with individual shower heads and hoses that sprayed Dr. Bronner's soap foam and water, in the middle of the woods with sixty strangers, male *and* female, all in the name of love and freedom. (Don't ask! I'll get into more detail about it in my next book.) I will say though, that it was fucking radical and liberating and freezing! My winky was the size of a mini-Charleston Chew, but it was well worth it, and it was the closest I have ever felt in my entire life to a group of people whom I barely even knew. Inhibitions can be crippling to us at times. They can drown us in distress and trap us in trepidation.

It's what makes grown-ups shudder at the idea of seeing someone else naked.

I can just see it now: A group of moms dropping their kids off at school, aghast at the site of a huge cock made of frozen particles that fell from the sky, whispering in shame, "Eww, gross. It's a penis. I haven't seen one of those since nine months before Tommy was born."

I don't understand this strange relationship we have developed with our sexuality, or lack thereof. I want to say that somewhere along the line, religious movements cast an ugly shadow over what was once considered amazing and beautiful. Naked bodies are fucking cool, man! I would really suggest—if you can find the time at some point in your life—that you hook up with a bunch of free-loving hippies, protest something you feel is oppressive to both yourself and humanity, and then get naked as the day you were born, together as a group. Just take it all off and let it swing like Mark McGuire, or Sammy Sosa, before he turned into that kid from the movie *Powder*. (I think I heard that joke somewhere before, but it's hilarious, so it's worth repeating.) But seriously, maybe start small and just sleep naked. Feel the cool sheets on your skin, experience freedom like never before. Then work your way up into walking around the house naked. Maybe go on a retreat into the desert and bare it all for the heavens. However you want to do it. Trust me. You will love it! And then you will learn to appreciate snow dicks just like me.

PS: I had to go outside with a shovel and dismember the penis like I was Lorena Bobbitt. I laughed out loud the entire time. And I have no doubt that the neighbors were peeking from behind drawn shades, disgusted at the thought of that dangerous, frozen dick.

Dear Parent,

Your child has thrown up not once, not twice, but three times this week. These were all separate incidents on different days, in the gym, the playground, and the hallway. I certainly don't want to be the one to pass judgment on your parenting technique, but I will point out that some things in life just aren't fucking cool.

Obviously, by sending your sick kid to school, you not only put other children in jeopardy, but you also set a bad example for your child by modeling that life is about you and only you, and everyone else can fuck off. I understand that you might have to work and that maybe you are a single parent—or maybe you are married, but your husband or wife is a dickhead and won't step up to the plate—but at the end of the day, money doesn't hold more value than human life, and as all of us working folk know, there is never enough anyway! Ever. Me love you long time. Please, keep that little one home next time and let them heal. Cheers!
Always,
Timbo

23

While the Cat's Away the Mice Will...Change Lightbulbs

Yes! This is what custodians live for! Days like this make it all worth it: an empty building free of students and faculty asking us to clean this or empty that or find this or pick up that. This is the epitome of custodial nirvana. No vomiting. No spills. No calls to move furniture or floods in the hallways. No lunchroom noise or candy wrappers thrown on the floor. It's just serenity and snow. Lots and lots of snow.

Everybody loves a snow day. It's like getting a free ride in the back of a car being driven by the Dalai Lama, Jim Morrison, and Prince, the coolest fucker on the planet and one of the greatest guitar players ever, to pick up a winning lottery ticket that you didn't pay for while getting a massage and a happy ending if you're into that sort of thing. It's what we lived for as kids. If you grew up in a geographical location that produces snow during the winter season, then you know that a snow day, on which school is cancelled due to inclement weather, is a reason to celebrate. You have the option to either hunker down inside and watch some flicks, all warm and fuzzy underneath the blankets, or you can opt to be adventurous by grabbing a sled and hitting up the nearest hill. Either way, you are free from the burden of school. There is not a single person on the planet who would prefer to sit in a classroom over sitting on the couch with their family while the ground gets covered in a white blanket of joy. That sounds like the beginning of a corny Christmas movie. (Keep me in mind,

Hallmark, I may need a job as a writer once I unleash this masterpiece into the stratosphere!)

While I no longer get to stay home on snow days unless it's too dangerous to drive to work, I do appreciate the solitude that comes along with pushing a snowblower around the school property perimeter or shoveling out steps and entranceways while most people are inside their homes. There is freedom in being alone while the snow falls.

Out of our three-man crew, two of us usually use the snow machines and one of us takes a shovel and digs out doorways and steps. I am the youngest and low man on the totem pole as far as years on the job go, so usually I work the shovel, but I don't mind. It's an opportunity for some exercise, and it makes me feel like I am in the movie *Rocky IV* when Rocky travels to Russia to train for his fight against Ivan Drago. Seriously, it is the best Rocky movie out of all of them. Don't be a lame ass and tell me that the first one is. Yes, the original *Rocky* is great, but nothing tops the fight with the Russian. And the soundtrack is fresh. Plus, a young Brigitte Nielsen is in it as well. I rest my case.

On the days when the snow continues to fall, we take trips around the outside of the building every hour or so to keep the snow from becoming too heavy, and then in between we complete certain tasks like changing lightbulbs, fixing things that need some fixing, and other general maintenance stuff. It is nothing exciting, but in some weird way, it allows the job to be different for a little bit, or sort of different, and above all else, quiet. Quiet is good. Good for the soul, a challenge for the mind.

On the flip side of the coin, some winters are brutal and feel like they will never end. When the snow keeps coming, and the temperature refuses to rise above twenty degrees it starts to make you lose your mind a little bit. The dark days wear on the soul, leading it down a path that craves the sun and springtime sounds, kids on bikes, and the warm afternoons and cool nights while new life begins to pop up. When this takes place, everyone knows the summertime is right around the corner, waiting to jump out like a stripper in a birthday cake. Being from the Northeast is pretty rewarding in that the winter makes you work your ass off in order to reap the reward of the summertime sky, and you also get to experience all four seasons in their entirety.

During the winter, it is the ice that makes it painstakingly tedious. Once the ground freezes over the only thing we can do is put down rock salt and sand, chop at it with metal picks and shovels, and hope to God that the temperature doesn't warm up and then drop again. When that happens, any snow on the ground turns into water and then back into ice, and it makes life around here pretty irritating. Chop, chop, chop, breathe. Chop, chop, chop, breathe.

Because our society has grown accustomed to suing the crap out of one another every chance we get, as custodians we need to be sure that we leave no chance for someone to slip and fall. We work our asses off to ensure that everyone walking on school grounds during the winter still has the opportunity to look down at their cell phone while they drop their kid off, instead of actually paying attention so they don't slip and break their neck. It is also interesting to note that when we decide to sue a school district, police force, etc., or anything attached to a system of government, we are in essence suing ourselves because the state takes our tax money to pay out the people who are doing the suing. You have to admit that it is clever on their part, and it's safe to say they got us by the balls every which way we turn. So next time you bust your ass on some ice because you are looking at pictures of cats on your phone instead of paying attention, make sure you don't sue your neighbor, or yourself for that matter.

For the duration of the school year, it is our job to have the school open by seven o'clock in the morning. What that means is that anytime there is snow or ice on the ground, we arrive at the very least two hours before teachers do, sometimes even more. By five in the morning we have already begun making sure the grounds are safe for faculty, students, and parents. When the snow falls, we pick it up, and when it falls again, we pick it up again, and when the ice forms, we do our job with due diligence to remove it, and despite all of our efforts, it goes almost without fail that someone, somewhere, will complain that it wasn't done "enough." Someone will call and say that there was still ice on this sidewalk or not enough salt on that sidewalk, or that there was a puddle in the walkway that they had to walk around. There have been times when board of education members have taken pictures of ice they saw and brought it directly to the superintendent's office, doing their best to beat their chests and make sure that we, the lowly custodians, know their roles. Through it all, we continue to shovel shit, work when no one else is working, and smile even when we are in the right, instead of telling some people to grow the fuck up and find some sense of purpose.

What we see from this point of view is that most "adults" need a caretaker. They need someone to dump their unhappiness on, and they need a reason to feel special, and many still need someone to pick up after them and make sure their paths are clear. What easier way to feel powerful and important than to try your hardest to get the neighborhood custodian in trouble because he may have missed a little ice while he was freezing his dick off in the pitch dark at five in the morning? No matter, we do our thing, collect our checks, and live to fight—I mean clean—another day. I'm not bitter, just passionate. Don't confuse the two.

It's beginning to look a lot like Christmas. Dear summer, hurry.

* We should allow our kids to learn about the quiet more often. Not the type of quiet in which an entire class sits and works on something silently, but the type of quiet that allows children to learn about their own inner workings and explore their subconscious minds. If we do this, it will give them the tools to grow into an awareness that doesn't exist in this type of social setting. They will certainly start to "get it" once they begin to explore the void inside.

Do yourself a favor next time it snows. Go outside and listen to the quiet. Now you're living.

This lunchroom is a cross between *One Flew Over the Cuckoo's Nest, Romper Room,* and the TV show *Oz.* Hey, Jesus of Nazareth, now's a good time for you to come back and work some miracles... WTF?

24

Summertime and the Living Is Easy, Unless You Work in a Fifties-Era Building with No Air Conditioning

It's only 8:00 a.m. and already I am sweating like I am having a panic attack in the middle of a volcano. The air is thick, humid, unforgiving. As the days pass, it only gets hotter because the summer heat sits still, waiting for you to walk through it, daring you to try to find safety from its cruelty. There is nowhere to escape to and nowhere to hide. Opening windows does very little to alleviate the stifling air and usually only allows an even hotter breeze to waft in, feeling like a blow-dryer on the back of my neck. It makes me want to take all my clothes off and eat some mushrooms and start singing, "This is the dawning of the Age of Aquarius," but I don't. I just work. As my shirt sticks to my skin, the sweat beads into my mouth and burns my eyes, and I simply block it out and work. It is challenging and (insert your adjective here). *Where my Mad Libs peeps at?*

Comedian Dane Cook referred to the DMV as Satan's asshole, but I can assure you, this building in the middle of the summer is the real Satan's asshole, and it stinks. Even the asbestos-tainted tiles sweat, emitting their poisonous perspiration into the greasy summer days, and through it all, from June 30 until Labor Day weekend, while teachers and students are roaming free, swimming, laughing, eating, and dreading the ever-present gloom of returning back to school, we, the caretakers, are hard at work cleaning every single nook and cranny of this old building: every desk, chair, window, blind, curtain, bookshelf, computer, floor, bathroom, and wall. Every carpet, mirror, step, handrail, radiator, and light—it *all* gets cleaned and polished, waxed and shined, fixed and secured. We paint and move furniture over and over and over again, and we do it all knowing that by the end of the first week of school it will all be spilled on, stepped on, pissed on, puked on, and in some cases even shit on. It is perhaps the most unrewarding outcome known to man. We break our backs for ten weeks straight, save for a week or two of vacation, daydreaming about being at the beach with our kids and families and knowing the inevitable is near: everything we cleaned will be dirty again, and much of it dirty as the result of another human being's carelessness.

It's not all depressing, though. Like snow days, the summer weeks are quiet. I use my break times to play ball in the gym or work out on the playground: push-ups, pull-ups, jump rope, body squats, handstands. You know, real ninja shit. We play music every day in the halls, we curse out loud, and we choose which faculty bathroom we are individually going to commandeer for the long months ahead. We laugh a lot at how fucked-up the world is and talk about how much time we have left before retiring or moving on to greener pastures, just like people do in prison, but above all else, we sweat and swear, clean and curse.

Every so often I climb up on the roof, black as night with tar, littered with baseballs, tennis balls, and other round objects, to soak up a little bit of summer sun and get some alone time. I stare up and out into the distance, thinking about life and why it has taken me to this exact moment or why I am fortunate enough to still be alive, and how when I truly find those peaceful seconds I see that beneath all the human interference, the world truly is magnificent. And as much as I hate this gig most days, it's not all that bad because somewhere, someone else is suffering, and I'm not. I'm just working an unfulfilling job, and that's not the end of the world.

In most schools during the summer, the district will hire what is referred to as "summer help." Summer help is a group of high school students who have the option to be gainfully employed during their most precious of free times in order to make a little cash. And when I say a little cash, I mean a very, very, very small amount of cash. Some districts have even begun offering students a half credit toward their diplomas if they choose to participate in the summer help program. It's a clever way to introduce kids to the workforce and get them used to what most people think life is really about: working, making some money, paying taxes, buying a house, driving a car, reading the morning paper, fearing the terrorists, settling for the status quo. And being that the job is so banal, it usually takes the kids who get hired about a week or so before they realize what they actually signed up for. They also do not get their first paycheck until about a month after they begin working, so their obvious enthusiasm on the first day slowly fades into sluggishness and despair as the days go by while they wait for their first paycheck.

Normally that first check only clears about a hundred dollars. The kids open it with excitement, frantically studying every number, and I always find it interesting to see how most of the time, their first reaction is, "This is bullshit." Questions like "Why do they take so much money out of my check?" or "How come I didn't get paid for a full two weeks when I've been working for three already?" uttered with a sense of frustration and defeat, lead to overall attitudes of "fuck this job" and "who gives a shit?" Any bit of work ethic they may have brought with them into the job quickly dissolves, and for the most part the summer helpers come in, do a half-ass job for six to eight weeks and go back to school in the fall, completing their 365-day cycle of never leaving a school building.

Come to think of it, when it's put in that context—that these kids are spending most of their time in a school building year round—it only makes sense that the idea of *not* buying into the rat-race life would seem foreign to them.

Maybe if we advised students to *not* go to college right away, to instead focus on trying to work a job to make some money while they pursue things they are truly passionate about, like building their own business or creating something new, with the assurance that college will always be there, whether now or later, will allow them to develop a richer understanding of how our monetary system works—i.e., debt and interest and the "taking out a loan" trap. Maybe then these young adults can decide if college is right for them. I bet if we stopped pouring the idea of college down kids' throats like a funnel at a keg party, they would begin to see that paying thousands upon thousands upon thousands of dollars for an education is in actuality the opposite of smart, it's fucking dumb, and shameful, *and* a complete scam. And something that needs to change.

I was a summer worker when I was a kid. Even then the job was the same. I can remember the way the days would drag, how the buildings had that unique institutional smell to them, like being trapped in an empty mental ward, the hallways lacking only wheelchairs and drooling patients and nurses with Dixie cups and a handful of pills. I felt like Brad Pitt in the movie *12 Monkeys*, only I wasn't making any money, and Bruce Willis was nowhere to be found. In retrospect, even then I knew that I had to get out, and I did for a little bit, but now I'm back. Shit.

It is very interesting to see that at thirty-six years old, my joyous and tortured soul, which has already jumped and ducked, bobbed and weaved, and risen and fallen enough for two lifetimes, has made its way back to the establishment that we call "education." Life is a cold, ironic dickface sometimes, but it's the kind of dickface you just want to hug and thank, even though it kicks the living crap out of you. Watching these young kids work during the summer, wondering to myself if any of them will ever truly live out their dreams—or more important, find real happiness—observing that I was them once and they might be me one day, is something that sticks in my gut and lights a fire in my heart. It makes me want to keep fighting the crooks and keep standing up for equality.

When July 1 hits and the district sends us our summer helpers, I make it a point to give these kids a different view on life. I make sure that I am setting an example of what I think it should be. Fuck fear. Do *you*, kid. Follow your dreams, your path, and your will. That paycheck that you just opened, the one that you were bitching about because the government stole half of it, that will *never* make it to your grave, so do your very best to free yourself from what *we*, the frightened adults in your world, have been planting in your brain your entire life. It isn't what you have been told, rather it is what you haven't been told. Simply put: believe. Summertime and the living is easy…but not around here.

25

Bros, Brahs, and the Language behind Education

recently heard a teacher say to a student, "We are in school now so we are educated. We do not use words like *bro* when we speak." Well, shit, if that's the case then I must be an ignoramus. Truthfully, my ego wanted to take what I heard personally, as if that teacher was talking directly to me, and insulting me, you know, the me who believes himself to be special and unique. But alas, I have come too far to fall into that trap. It wasn't personal and never is. They were simply words from the mind of another human being, BUT it did get me to thinking, so I took it to task in my mind and heart and began to slowly decipher what it means to be "educated" in the minds of some.

I use the word *bro* all the time. In the environment in which I was raised, using the word *bro* at the end of every sentence was about as normal as saying hello when picking up the phone. It is good to note further that on the West Coast, people use an altered version of the term in the form of *bruh* or *brah*. For example:

East Coast: "What's up, bro?"
West Coast: "What's up, brah?"

I personally use the West Coast version more than the East Coast version because it fits my style better. *Bro* tends to come off with a bit more aggressiveness, and *bruh* has a laid-back quality to it, and believe it or not,

I am pretty laid-back, regardless of what conclusions you've drawn about my personality thus far.

So what does it mean to be educated? Certainly we can't automatically assume that just because someone goes to school or graduates from college with a degree that they are therefore educated. After all, George Bush graduated from Yale and Harvard, and I think we can all agree that he is certainly not the cleanest mop in the closet. (Yeah, yeah, I know, that was an awful attempt at humor on my part. So what?)

People have long associated going to school with being educated. Because there has never been another way in which to gauge education, people have no choice but to believe that gaining an education can only happen in the form of traditional schooling, like college or grad school. Since most children are in a certain type of school setting by the age of five, or maybe even younger if we consider prekindergarten, then it is easy to see why as they grow into adults they have an unwavering belief that going to school is the way to become educated. Dictionary.com defines education as:

the act or process of imparting or acquiring general knowledge, developing the powers of reasoning and judgment, and generally of preparing oneself or others intellectually for mature life.

You will notice that the word *school* is nowhere to be found in this definition. What is found though are the words *reasoning* and *judgment*, two attributes that have seemingly flown out the goddamn window in the long and tattered history of public schooling.

If reasoning and judgment are considered the "powers" behind education, then how is it that the driving force behind public school reasoning is the belief that because kids are of the same age, then they should therefore learn at the same pace? It's like we have gone from warp speed to ludicrous speed and forgotten that Rick Moranis is one of the funniest actors of all time. Totally off topic but it fired off one of my neurons so I wrote it. Fuck it. The point is that an education can be obtained from so many facets of life and carrying the staunch belief that "schooling" is the only way to truly become educated is…wait for it…ludicrous! Yes! I knew it would connect somehow! (Please reference the movie *Spaceballs* if you are confused.)

Words are merely words, and culture simply defines how those words will be perceived. What matters more? That a kid said "bro" to one of his classmates, or that his teacher made him believe he was uneducated for saying it? You know what I think. Catch ya lata, bruh.

26

If You Want to Teach, Teach, or Keep Bitching About Teachers Having the Summer Off—Either Way, Shut Your Trap

Let's face it. Teachers get a bad rap. It's easy to see why. To the outside world, anyone who only works 180 days of the year—has off every single holiday known to the civilized world except maybe Arbor Day; spends ten weeks off every summer; doesn't do any type of manual labor except move a desk once in a while or carry a few reams of paper to the copy machine; starts the day at eight and is done by three if they choose to be, and in some regions of the country makes a very decent salary that includes paid sick time, personal and family benefits, union protection, and discounts with outside services—has the life. A large percentage of us work year round and have to put in many years before we build up paid vacation time and the like, and it is understandable why those of us who work year-round might sneer at teachers when they complain about how hard their job is.

With regard to the aspects named above, teachers do certainly have "the life," *but* it should be understood that the reason teachers have all of these perks is because they chose to be teachers. People who complain that educators are afforded too much should accept responsibility for their decisions to not become teachers and maybe reconsider their current professions. It should be made clear that what teachers do is by no means easy. Most of us can't make it through the day without wanting to put duct tape across our kids' mouths and string them up on the roof, so imagine what it's like to have to deal with twenty or more kids a day who aren't even yours! They don't even share the same genetic makeup, for Christ's sake! Teachers have to deal with all of the shit that comes along with students whose parents might have mental issues or are drug addicts, divorced, abusive, absentee, or unsupportive. On top of that, they have to follow rules and guidelines and whatever other crap the Department of Education chooses to shove onto their desks.

A disproportionate number of students in public schools require special attention, students who are not capable of learning in the type of setting a classroom can offer. The assumption that all children are capable of learning at the same pace simply because they are the same age is absolutely asinine. There are so many outside factors, so many intangibles in each student's personal life that no matter what act of Congress we pass, like No Child Left Behind, there will always be children left behind in one way or another. I've said it before, and I'll say it again, the public education model is completely flawed.

LOST IN THE SYSTEM

Beth has Asperger's syndrome, and for the four years that she has been in public school, nobody has diagnosed her as such or told her family that this may be a possibility. Not one school psychologist or social worker, not one doctor or nurse, has come to that conclusion.

Beth began her stint in public school in kindergarten. She struggles with everything and has a hard time dealing with other kids. She is constantly disruptive, making her teacher's job nearly impossible on some days. Often, while her teacher is instructing, Beth will get up, walk around the classroom, run out of the room, yell at her classmates, and generally prevent the class lessons from running smoothly. To reiterate, she has been doing this for over four years.

Beth needs a different setting. She needs personalized attention and one-on-one instruction. She also needs a better home life: parents who show up more, parents who aren't themselves struggling with social communication. She has none of this. Beth does not have anything that she needs to move forward in life and evolve, and the school system is just fine with that, or at the very least, complacent.

The state does not give a shit about Beth or her classmates or her teacher. The state cares about its money and its power. The teacher and students bear the brunt of all this incompetence, and when Beth doesn't do well on her Common Core standardized test this year, her teacher and fellow students will reap the outcome. When the other students struggle to do well because Beth has been disrupting *every single lesson* that has been taught this year, the teacher will be punished, given a bad rating or deemed ineffective. There is something missing here. A part of the equation has gone astray and the wealth behind the scenes trumps the need to fill in the empty puzzle piece. Beth is the puzzle piece, her classmates are the puzzle, and her teacher is the box trying to hold all the pieces together in one place. The system will not let us pass go but will gladly collect our $200.

The reality is that this happens *all the time*. Every day there is a child lost in the mix, swimming against the current, needing badly to be met in the middle so his or her special needs can be fully attended to, and it simply does not happen. It's not only in schools but outside as well. There is no law in place that says you are not allowed to have children. There are laws in place that attempt to hold parents accountable for their actions when it comes to the health and safety of their children, but unfortunately, it is impossible to keep children safe simply by threatening with the rule of law. We all hear horrific stories involving children and wonder how or why. When someone who has children is so far removed from their own love and carries pain so deeply, the child will always wind up as the unfortunate victim.

There is a pervasive theme throughout the world that plays out in regard to children and parents, and many times that theme is: Parents raise their children in an unhealthy environment because they were raised the same way. Many adults take on their parents' mental and emotional baggage. They add some more of their own pain into that baggage and then dump that heavy old suitcase on the backs of their children.

Because a lot of kids spend a majority of their time in school, the responsibility of helping them through emotional confusion, anger, resentment, etc., falls on the teachers and faculty provided to them. If parents are not concerned with how their children are behaving and are not reinforcing what it is to keep healthy boundaries, appreciate others, respect your community, speak kindly, or dream passionately (all things teachers should be adding into their curriculum daily), then how are students supposed to evolve with such inconsistent and counterproductive home and school environments? This is the reason students like Beth get lost. It is the reason so many children are frustrated and afraid of what an average school day is going to bring their way. What most of us see as human lives, the system only sees as numbers. Beth is yet another digit, gliding down the conveyor belt, picked up, taken apart, reassembled, and dropped again, year after year after year.

27

Ahh! The Redcoats Are Coming!

I've been at work for an hour and forty-five minutes, and four different people have already told me, "The superintendent is coming!"

I'm fascinated. What is it about the work environment that makes people cower in fear when they hear the boss coming to visit? Why do some people display a noticeable sense of anxiousness, as if they have a target on their back that says, "I'm incompetent. Please don't fire me!"

I have never met the superintendent. I have only heard about her, minor mutterings about the type of person she is. "She's nice; she's one of us; she's different. She really cares about her job." This may all be true, and I hope it is. I am not in the position to form any type of opinion on this matter, as I have no firsthand knowledge of who she is. I do know this: She is a person just like me, so any idea of me being afraid that she might judge me or the job I am doing is just that—an idea. It is an unreality to me. I work the same way no matter who is visiting our building. Same job, different day. If you are confident in your abilities and honest with yourself, if you are kind and generous and compassionate, then looking another human being in the eye and consciously letting them know we are on the same human level becomes first nature. Whether we're the president, Garth Brooks, Pee Wee Herman, or Jay Z, *we are all on the same level.* Don't let anyone convince you otherwise. The sooner we comprehend this as a global society, the sooner we evolve closer toward peace.

We can no longer afford to believe that a certain title defines someone as greater than or lesser than. People are people, and success is whatever you want it to be. With that said:

"Good morning to you, Mrs. Superintendent. My name is Tim. It's nice to meet you."

Apparently, a few students in room 105 have pinkeye. Awesome. I can't wait to clean that room. Jesus, Mary, Joseph, Mohammed, and whoever the fuck else humanity has decided to name God, next time around can you take pinkeye, ringworm, and lice out of the equation? Seriously, I'll be eternally grateful. Cheers!

28

Defender of Cleanliness, Liberator of Blockages

It is safe to say there is not a custodian alive who can match my skills with a plunger! Clogged toilet, you say? *Boom, zap, pang!* I'll have that dirty bitch flushing the right way before you even have a chance to wipe your ass! I am a creature of the night. I lurk in the shadows and hide in the trash receptacles. I am so obscure that I blend in with the dust on the shelves and sleep in the cobwebs. When you pull out a paper towel, I am literally hiding inside of the dispenser making sure that nothing gets jammed. I brush my teeth with hand soap and tighten my dreadlocks up with floor wax. I can morph into a desk or transform into a ladder. Vomit, gone; urine in the radiator, bollocks; moldy sandwich hidden in the back of a desk, yummy. Dinner. I am the night porter and I am king.

Look no further…

29

Flying Dragons, Master Locks, and Barbed Wire

Eleven o'clock Monday night. Springtime. Cool breeze. Perfection. Clear sky. Half moon. The earth speaks in silence. I walk. Three steps down the side entrance to the outside world. It's just me and the gods and goddesses. Time to secure this building. Proclaim it safe for the evening. Then go home to my warm bed and beautiful wife, like a native returning from a hunt, exhausted but ready for anything.

I turn to my left and grab the two garbage cans that only three hours earlier were completely empty but are now completely full. There is so much trash. What are we doing to this planet? Don't think about it. Just work. The wheels on which the cans are sitting roll like an old man moves: creaking, squeaking, and stumbling. I guide them, one hand on each, on autopilot, cool as can be. That breeze, though, yes, you can't beat it. Into the shed they go. Like bodies piling up, garbage bags overflow, crushing each other to death, suffocating on their own plastic. The one closest to the front has a hole chewed in the side of it with crumbs trailing off. My friend the squirrel was here again today, right around lunch, smart little bugger. I smile to myself inside my mind; it's personal, not for anyone else to see. Animals see the value in food. If only we were all squirrels.

I shut the shed door, pulling down on it with all my might. The shed is relatively new, but for some reason the door doesn't work quite right. It's a good thing I can channel Bruce Lee when I need to. Bruce always has the strength to get the crappy shed door closed. Be water, my friend. Be dirty water in a mop bucket if you have to, but either way, be water. Turn handle. Shed closed. Garbage away. Next.

Head north toward the playground and the field. The building is on my left, towering like a castle out of *Game of Thrones*. A dragon flies overhead, shooting fire and squealing. Just kidding. But that would be the tits. The nighttime lights are on, illuminating the side parking lot, making sure kids aren't hovering in the dark, smoking weed and drinking shitty beer like my friends and I did growing up. We were pros. These kids nowadays are nothing but amateurs. Come here, kid, let the janitor show you how it's done.

All windows are shut tight. No wait, is that one open? Shit, room 211. Damn it. I always miss that one. Mental note. Close window in room 211 when you go back inside, don't forget. Keep walking. Deep breath. Life is fresh. Here comes the playground on the right. I hear the sound of a car passing on the back street. *Whoosh.* Hmm. Wonder who it is. Where they are going? Where they are coming from? Are they happy? Do they want to be? Am I?

Playground is clear. The monkey bars are calling my name. Okay, monkey bars, I will oblige. Thirty pull-ups, you say? Sounds good to me. Either the neighbors admire my commitment to you every time they see us do this dance, or they are pissed off that their tax dollars are going toward my vanity and physique. Twenty-eight, twenty-nine, thirty. See you tomorrow, my friend. Don't be late.

To the kindergarten entrance we go. Door one, locked. Door two, locked. Smooth. I turn left around the corner of the building; the field is on my right. Heading west now. The field is the size of the Mojave Desert. Actually, I could throw a rock across it if I wanted to, but the Mojave Desert sounds slick, like James Dean or James Gandolfini, depending on what you're in to. I walk up two steps and yank on the two fifth-grade entrance doors. Locked. Locked. No sweat. Peace out, fifth grade. See ya tomorrow. Moving on.

Look up. Orion's Belt, Little Dipper. Another car drives by. I hear the muffled sound of music—Reggaeton, to be exact. The muffler is blasting.

Whoosh. Gone. And I am back to the silence. Yes. Thank you, Baby Jesus. Across the field the back fence stands tall. The only thing it is missing is barbed wire. It doesn't necessarily mean you are not in jail just because you can't see the bars. Twenty years until retirement. The state says I owe them thirty more dollars for my taxes this year. I say they owe *us* our lives. Breathe, Tim. You got this. One, two, three. Good. Put one foot in front of the other and marvel at the wonder of walking. How is this happening? What makes my legs move like this? Weird, but incredible.

Here is the courtyard. Need to lock this gate. Make sure no one can get in. We all lock one another out. We place restrictions on it all. Our fears and emptiness lead to permanently silent courtyards. Note to self: My courtyard will never be locked. All are welcome.

There is sand everywhere. It was a long winter, lots of snow. There is also sand in Florida. That would be nice right about now. Look around. All windows secured. I'm on point tonight. Except for 211. Crap, get over it, Tim. The desert reappears, only this time it is the desert I went to in Northern California a few years back. It changed me. I didn't eat for three weeks. I was free. It was the greatest thing I've ever done. Shoot. Wrong book. Save it.

The pavement is cracking from the water underneath, expanding, re-tracting. This is where the kids get their free time to run and play, kick, jump, throw, and fly. It's the yard. They get a half hour every lunch period. I think in the county correctional center, inmates get an hour a day. Damn. Sorry, kids. Dream big.

Pull the gates shut. They scrape against the ground and struggle to stay open. Not tonight, gate. I'm running the show, and you're closing whether you like it or not. Master lock open, chain wraps around, clank, clink, click. Locked down. Halfway done. Am I halfway done with life or with securing the building? Who knows? Either way, I'm at peace.

Still heading west. The "greatest city in the world" is only about thirty miles from here. Maybe I should just keeping walking. I can get there by sunrise. Remember that time you walked from Brooklyn to Washington, DC? It only took two weeks. Damn it, dude, that's for another book as well.

One, two steps up to the first set of gym doors. All good. It's only fifteen yards to the next set. Make sure to check this one good, 'cause sometimes it looks closed but isn't. Yep, closed as well. Closed in Spanish is *cerrado*. Good job, man. Keep *practicando*. Down the wheelchair-accessible ramp to the bottom. You're lucky; you can walk. Don't ever forget that. Ever. Make a left.

It's a beautiful night out here. That plane is loud but really high. I used to be loud and really high all the time. Chuckle, chuckle. Put that in your book. Done. Next set of doors, heading south now. South is where the ocean is. South is where we will be in another eight weeks, surfing, sunning, bumming, and being. I. Can't. Wait. The entrance to the lobby is good to go. I can't believe how many cars we cram into this narrow parking lot during the day. Suburbia goes...minivan, SUV, minivan, SUV, minivan, Hyundai. Someone always has a Hyundai. My friend Lou had a Hyundai once. We used to take it to Manhattan so we could groove out all night. Break-dancing, house dancing, music, sweat, and *love*. Best times of my life. Ha! I danced professionally once. That's crazy. Now I'm a custodian—a dancing custodian. There are eighteen windows on this side of the building. Closed. Excellent. No need to come back over here. Heading into the homestretch. Make another left, start moving east. East is where life begins. East is the element of fire. The natives had it right.

The main entrance is nothing special. Just two doors made up of metal, glass, and some other material I can't describe. Three steps up. Jump up them! There are only three, dude. Go for it. You're a tiger ready to pounce. Go! Made it. But damn, that left ankle is still shaky. Grab handles. Yank. Locked. Back down to the sidewalk. Just a few weeks ago this was covered in ice. Now, clear as can be. East, east, east, look up at the flagpole, damn you, day-shift guys, you forgot to take the flag down. I got it, but don't make it a habit. Wait, look left. All windows on this side closed, cafeteria lights off, sitting pretty like a model in a magazine. Back to the flag I go. I wonder if someone is watching me, ready to tell me that I better not let the flag touch the ground. Nearly three million children under the age of five starve to death every year in this world, and you're worried about a piece of cloth touching the ground? Get your priorities straight, asshole. The flag comes down without incident. I used to be in Cub Scouts when I was a kid. Hilarious. One more set of doors to check, safe and secure. Another left turn, and I am back where I started, staring at the aluminum shed, approaching the side entrance, the portal into the underworld of my daily existence. Outside property all clear. A few last things before I leave and drive off into the night listening to Keith Hudson, the dark prince of reggae, dreaming about Venice Beach, my family, my autonomy, my security, my *real* life, not my job life.

Upstairs hallway lights, off. Downstairs hallway lights, off. Beautiful aquatic friends with fins, fed. Office lights, off. Personal belongings, gathered. Time to make my daily escape. Rejoice!

I'm ready to chase those outer- world dreams once again; : the tax-free dreams, the dreams that are mine to make, the dreams that I see in the eyes of my kids, the dreams that I pray to see in the eyes of these students. Alarm box, beep, beep, beep, beep. Exit delay in progress, counting down from thirty, alarm engaged. Yes. Alarm engaged. Yes! Good night, building. See ya soon! Teachers, students, faculty, your building is safe, secure, and most of all, clean. I'm sure that will not be the case by nine o'clock tomorrow morning, so enjoy it while it lasts. Good night.

Change the world before it changes you.

30

Later Is Now, and Then You're Gone

Tick, Tock, Alive, Awake, in Conclusion

The problem does not lie with one group. It is not *only* the teachers' fault or the students' fault or the parents' fault. Believe it or not, it isn't even entirely the lying bureaucrats' fault, although blaming it on shitty government policy and ridiculous oversight does make sense sometimes and sure as hell feels good. In reality, the fault lies in all of us together for our failure to wake up sooner to a different truth and a different set of principles.

Sure, we can continue on this path, wasting, blaming, hoping, fearing, and pretending we are doing a great job, *or* we can admit that we are screwing up in areas where we can't afford to screw up. First and foremost, by our blatant abuse and disrespect of the natural world around us, and second by our willingness to settle for a dismissive attitude that allows us to rationalize our shortcomings by saying, "It is what it is." No, it isn't. It is what we make it, so let's make it something worth fighting for. It all starts with communication, healthy communication, and ends with…well, I don't really know how it ends. That is up to us.

What I do know is that everything is fleeting. It is all a temporary fix. Every sunrise and sunset, every tick and every tock, and every moment that you live are all just experiences that we can only have in the present moment. The rest is just a matter of our minds. Memories and imaginations make up the lonely space inside our bat-shit-crazy heads. Let's take one gigantic conscious breath together and decide right *now* that we are going to make something better happen for our kids and for one another. We can do it. I know we can!

With that said, it has been real and fun, my friends. I had an awesome time writing what has mainly been a one-sided conversation with myself, and I truly hope you enjoyed reading this. Thanks so much for listening. Until next time, desire true freedom and be the real change.

Tim Will Hunting
March 2015

THE ESSENTIAL CUSTODIAL READING LIST

1. *Dharma Punx*—Noah Levine
2. *Siddhartha*—Hermann Hesse
3. *A People's History of the United States*—Howard Zinn
4. *The New Jim Crow*—Michelle Alexander
5. *A Fighter's Heart*—Sam Sheridan
6. *The Four Agreements*—Don Miguel Ruiz
7. *Shantaram*—Gregory David Roberts
8. *Lies My Teacher Told Me*—James W. Loewen
9. *Zealot*—Reza Aslan
10. *The Brazilian Jiu Jitsu Globetrotter*—Christian Graugart
11. *The Breakthrough*—Dr. Fred Hartman
12. *The Way of the Peaceful Warrior*—Dan Millman
13. *The Berenstain Bears and the Spooky Old Tree*—Stan and Jan Berenstain
14. *Rikki-Tikki-Tavi*—Rudyard Kipling
15. *The Evolution of a Cro-Magnon*—John Joseph
16. *The Laws of the Ring*—Urijah Faber
17. *The Answer to the Riddle Is Me*—David Stuart MacLean
18. *Saltwater Buddha*—Jaimal Yogis
19. *Live from Death Row*—Mumia Abu-jamal
20. *The Medicine Way*—Kenneth Meadows

I am also a pretty big fan of comic books. It takes an immense imagination and true talent to create certain visions through art, and that is why I dig them so damn much. It seems like the more acceptable grown-up term to refer to a comic nowadays is *graphic novel*, but seriously, it's a freakin' comic book. Get over it. Here are a few of my favorites.

American Vampire—Scott Snyder
Daredevil—Frank Miller
Spawn—Todd McFarlane

Batman—Frank Miller or Scott Snyder
30 Days of Night—Steve Niles
The Walking Dead—Robert Kirkman
Scalped—Jason Aaron
The Infinity Gauntlet—Jim Starlin
V for Vendetta—Alan Moore
Boxers & Saints—Gene Luen

About the Author

Tim Will Hunting, creator of the podcast and blog *The Custodian Chronicles,* has nearly fifteen years of experience working as a custodian in American public schools.

Born in the United States, he has numerous creative interests that involve music, dance, entertainment, and the written word. Lead singer for the alternative rock band The Native Alien Tribe, he has also released several hip-hop albums as a solo artist and has worked as a professional dancer and master of ceremonies throughout the tristate area for various entertainment companies.

Among his other skills, Hunting has been a longtime practitioner of the martial arts, specializing in Brazilian jiujitsu. He lives on Long Island, New York.

Made in the USA
Middletown, DE
21 February 2017